Heidemarie Böcker

Regensburg

A Guide to the UNESCO
World Heritage City

Verlag
Friedrich Pustet

4

Via Regensburg's green belt to the former monastery of
St Emmeram, from there through the Bachgasse to the Goldener
Turm, past Don Juan to Fischmarkt and the former Danube port, over
the Steinerne Brücke and the Wöhrd Islands to Stadtamhof. (Town plan
inside front cover)

From the north-eastern corner of the Roman fort to the
Porta Praetoria, from the Bischofshof via Watmarkt past the
Baumburgerturm to the Old and the New Town Halls, from Haidplatz,
the city's festival site, to the Temple of the Muses. (Town plan inside
front cover)

Bibliografische Information der Deutschen Nationalbibliothek
Die Deutsche Nationalbibliothek verzeichnet diese Publikation in der
Deutschen Nationalbibliografie; detaillierte bibliografische Daten
sind im Internet über http://dnb.d-nb.de abrufbar.

4th revised and enlarged edition 2009
ISBN 978-3-7917-2156-9
© 1998 by Verlag Friedrich Pustet
English translation: Alison and Susanna Thielecke, Regensburg
Front Cover: Cathedral and Stone Bridge (Steinerne Brücke)
Design (cover and text): 2design; Martin Veicht, Daniel Bastian
Production: Friedrich Pustet, Regensburg 2009

Route A

From the Suburbs to the Suburbs – from the Station to Stadtamhof

1. Ring of Avenues
2. Statue of King Ludwig I on Horseback
3. Castra Regina
4. Benedictine Monastery of St Emmeram***
5. Fürstliches Schloss**
6. Albrecht Altdorfer's House
7. Goldener Turm*
8. Kohlenmarkt
9. Fischmarkt
10. Runtingerhaus*
11. Kepler Memorial Museum
12. Am Wiedfang
13. Steinerne Brücke***
14. Salzstadel**
15. St Katharine's Hospital
16. St Mang's Church*

Route B

From East to West – following the Course of the Danube

17. Donaumarkt
18. Porta Praetoria**
19. Bischofshof
20. Baumburgerturm*
21. Goliathhaus*
22. New and Old Town Halls***
23. Fechtschulhof
24. Haidplatz**
25. Zum Goldenen Kreuz*
26. Arnulfsplatz
27. Velodrom

Route C

From West to East – right through the Centre

28. St Jakob's Church** with Schottenportal***
29. Bismarckplatz
30. Dominican Church of St Blasius*
31. Gymnasium Poeticum
32. Dreieinigkeitskirche*
33. Zant- and Ingolstetterhaus*
34. Neupfarrplatz
35. Haus Heuport**
36. Cathedral of St Peter***
37. St Ulrich's Church*
38. Niedermünster*
39. Alter Kornmarkt with Alte Kapelle***
40. Minoritenkirche*
41. Leerer Beutel*
42. Ostengasse
43. Ostentor*
44. Königliche Villa

What is more…

45. Walhalla**
46. Kelheim and the Befreiungs-halle**
47. Weltenburg Abbey** and the Danube Gorge
- (i) Tourist Information
- (S) Boat Trips
- (P) Multi-Storey Car Park
- (P) Underground Car Park
- (P) Car Park
- (WC) Public toilets
- World Heritage Area (central zone)

Regensburg – a City where Life is a Pleasure

Regensburg's 150,000 inhabitants make it the fourth-largest city in Bavaria today. It is ancient as far as its history is concerned (which is so significant that UNESCO added the whole of the old town, parts of the islands in the Danube, and Stadtamhof as well, to its World Heritage List in 2006); yet it is youthful because of its lifestyle. In contrast with many other city centres, the residents have not been ousted by office-workers; the historic centre still has more than 12,000 inhabitants. The healthy mixture of shops, offices, flats, hotels, restaurants, cafés and discotheques keeps the city centre lively, on working days and holidays, in the day time as well as at night. And is it because of the Roman heritage that life mainly takes place outdoors? The moment the first sunbeam appears, the people here indulge in the almost Mediterranean habit of setting up tables and chairs outside cafés and restaurants, both in the narrow alleys and in the many squares. This way of life is obviously savoured by Regensburg's inhabitants, who are full of joie de vivre, as well as by visitors from all over the world. Commerce and culture, hospitality and shops, bustle and peace... all of these may be found and enjoyed in the city centre in great variety.

Breakfasting outdoors in Regensburg's ancient city centre

The City's Location

Regensburg lies by a sharp bend in the Danube, the northernmost point of this, the second-longest river in Europe. Inside the city

The whole city centre at one glance

boundaries the river divides into two branches, which flow around two islands, the Upper and the Lower Wöhrd; a canal was constructed to the north of the river in 1973.

The city lies on latitude 49° 01' 14" and longitude 12° 05' 57" at a height of between 326 and 471 m above sea level. It covers an area of 80 km², of which the city centre takes up only 1.15 km².

Regensburg is the capital of the Oberpfalz (Upper Palatinate) and seat of the district government; since 1965 it has also been a university city, besides having a polytechnic, an university of church music and musical education, about 80 schools, including the cathedral choir school, which places an emphasis on music, and many other institutions of further education. Regensburg is twinned with Aberdeen, Bressanone, Clermont-Ferrand, Odessa, Pilsen and Tempe/Arizona.

In economic terms Regensburg is home to both trade and industry. 100,000 people are employed in the fields of electronics, light engineering, vehicles, trade, services and building; firms such as Siemens, BMW and Toshiba operate factories here.

The city lies at the junction of the major motorways A 3 (Frankfurt – Vienna) and A 93 (Munich – Hof), and it is also accessible by train or ship (via the Main-Danube-Canal or the river itself). The nearest airports are at Munich and Nuremberg. To the north-east, Regensburg is surrounded by the foothills of the Bavarian Forest, which is part of the biggest area of forest in Europe, known as 'Europe's green roof', from the north to the south-east by the Franconian hills and in the south and south-east by the fertile plain called the Gäuboden, where corn and sugar-beet are plentiful. Two rivers flow into the Danube just before it reaches Regensburg, the Schwarze Laber and the Naab, while a third, the Regen, has its confluence within the city boundaries, all three in turn or together cause the floods which occur regularly in the riverside areas of the city and are carefully documented inside and outside the Historische Wurstküche, the quaint old restaurant beside the ancient stone bridge on the Danube.

Chronology of the Most Important Historical Dates

c. 90 A.D. *Establishment of a Roman cohort camp in Kumpfmühl*
179 A.D. *Completion of the legionary fort of Castra Regina during the reign of Emperor Marcus Aurelius*
mid-6th cent. *The Bavarians settle in the area of the fort with their ruling dynasty, the Agilolfing dukes*
2nd half of the 7th cent. *Christianization of the Bavarians by the itinerant bishops Emeram and Erhard*
739 *Regensburg is made a bishopric*
788 *Tassilo III is captured by Charlemagne and deposed as Bavarian duke; Bavaria becomes part of Charlemagne's empire*
c. 900 *First extension of the city boundaries*

1135 – 1146 *Construction of the Steinerne Brücke (Stone Bridge)*
1245 *Regensburg becomes a free imperial city*
1274 *Building operations begin on the Gothic cathedral and the town hall of the city*
c. 1300 *Second extension of the city*
1486 – 92 *The impoverished city gives up its free imperial city status and subordinates itself to the Duke of Bavaria, who is however forced by the Emperor to relinquish Regensburg*
1519 *The Jews are held responsible for the desperate financial situation and are driven from the city, the ghetto is destroyed. Following a 'miracle', the Pilgrimage of the Beautiful Virgin begins, but ends again abruptly after an outbreak of the plague*

Regensburg's Many Names

Although the Danube is Regensburg's 'high street', the river does not appear in its name. Instead, the city was called after the Regen, which flows into the Danube at this point. Castra Regina, the name of the Roman military camp was already derived from this river. Radaspona is the city's Celtic name, but this is first mentioned as late as A.D. 772.

Further, often puzzling names for this one city are used in literary sources: for instance Tiburnia – Tiburtina, Quadrata – Quartanis, Hyatospolis, Ymbrispolis, Germainsheim, Metropolis. Ratisbona, the mediaeval Latin form, has been preserved in the Italian-, Spanish- and French-speaking parts of the world.

1532 *The Constitutio Criminalis Carolina, the code of penal procedure drafted by Emperor Charles V, is passed by the imperial diet. This penal code remained in force for centuries with only small alterations*

1542 *The free imperial city converts to the Protestant faith, but the diocese and the monasteries remain intact*

1630 *Johannes Kepler dies in Regensburg*

1663 – 1806 *Perpetual Diet*

1803 – 1810 *Prince-primate Carl von Dalberg rules in Regensburg*

1838 *Regensburg becomes the seat of the government of the Oberpfalz*

1842 *Solemn inauguration of the Walhalla by King Ludwig I*

1859 *Regensburg is linked to the railway system*

1863 *Inauguration of the Befreiungshalle (Hall of Liberation) in Kelheim*

1967 *Foundation of the university*

1979 *Celebration of the 1800th anniversary of the founding of Castra Regina*

1989 *1250th anniversary of the bishopric of Regensburg*

1992 *Opening of the Main-Danube canal*

1995 *750th anniversary of Regensburg's becoming a free imperial city*

2005 *Cardinal Joseph Ratzinger, a professor at the University of Regensburg from 1969 to 1977, is elected Pope and adopts the name Benedict XVI*

2006 *Regensburg is included in the UNESCO World Heritage List*

Art, Culture and Commerce – Regensburg's History

When the Romans Reached the Danube

The Danube was the border, the natural 'limes' of the Roman Empire. Even in prehistoric times two important trade routes had intersected here at the most northerly point of the Danube: the route along or on the Danube from west to east and the north-south one, which crossed the Danube at a ford.

Regensburg's history began modestly. On a hill to the south of the present-day city, in Kumpfmühl, about 600 soldiers, whose duty it was to protect the northern border of the province of Raetia, manned a cohort fort which was erected in about 90 A.D., near the site of today's massive, towering church of St Wolfgang. When this fort was destroyed in the 2nd century A.D., presumably by the Marcomans, one officer must have hurriedly buried his money and jewellery to protect them from the approaching enemy; he hid them so thoroughly that they came to light only a few years ago during road construction work (today they are on show at the Historical Museum, p. 81).

We do not know why a massive legionary fort was built near the river to replace the destroyed cohort camp. We do know, however, that this military camp, which measured 450 m by 540 m

and was constructed from huge stone blocks, was completed in 179 A.D. This date can be established on the basis of two stone fragments of an inscribed stone tablet which were found about a hundred years ago in the vicinity of the fort's eastern gate. Though the actual date, 179 A.D., is not mentioned, it can be calculated precisely from the information the tablet gives, i.e. that Commodus, the son of the emperor Marcus Aurelius, was already in his second term of office as consul and had also been victorious as a military leader.

**Roman treasure-trove on show
at the Historical Museum**

Due to its solid construction the fort not only served as a safe haven for the 6,000 soldiers, it also survived for many centuries and formed the core of the first capital of Bavaria after the Romans had withdrawn.

What has been preserved of Roman Regensburg may be seen by walking along the former walls of the fort or taking part in a guided tour of the excavations below the church of Niedermünster (p. 68). But the Roman section of the Historical Museum (p. 81), in which many of the exhibits illustrate the extensive commercial connections in Roman times, bears particularly eloquent witness to the city's Roman past.

There are no dependable written sources that tell us exactly when (in the 5th or early 6th century) the Roman fort was abandoned – and due to this our knowledge about the following centuries is also vague. It is generally presumed that the remaining Roman population – soldiers, traders or farmers who were sufficiently daring or who had already formed permanent ties with the 'indigenous population' – stayed here and intermarried with the Bavarians, the Germanic tribe which had invaded the area by the middle of the 6th century.

**Porta Praetoria –
the north gate of the Roman fort**

Bavaria's First Capital: the Rule of the Agilolfing Dukes

In his biography of St Emmeram (written c. 772) Arbeo von Freising decribes Emmeram's route as a missionary from Poitiers via southern Germany to the Danube in Bavaria. And 'then he reached the town of Radaspona, which, constructed as it was from hewn blocks, had become the capital of this people. The duke of the Bavarians, the brave Theoto, ruled here at that time'. The town is also described as impregnable, protected by the Roman walls which had been preserved. It can no longer or not yet be proved whether major building work was done in this period.

The arts and crafts had already achieved a high standard at that time, as is proved by numerous articles of jewellery found at burial sites. The first written documents, in the form of liturgical manuscripts with illuminated initials, were also produced in the newly founded monasteries of christianized Bavaria, first and foremost at St Emmeram's.

Even at that time, the city was already surrounded by fertile arable land and vineyards. Fish ponds, animal enclosures and extensive woods existed, all of which were needed to supply a 'capital'. A bishopric since 739, the city developed into the political, spiritual and cultural centre of the Bavarian empire which stretched from Bolzano to the River Lech, including the High and the Low Tauern mountains, the river Melk and the Bohemian Forest.

The Age of the Carolingians and Regensburg's Rise as the City of Kings and Emperors

The reign of the Agilolfings ended abruptly in 788, when Charlemagne captured and deposed Tassilo III. With the aim of creating a Holy Roman Empire, he annexed Bavaria and turned Regensburg, which had until then been ruled by dukes, into a city of kings and emperors for the following centuries. During the reigns of King Ludwig the German (d. 876) and Emperor Arnulf of Carinthia (887–899), it even became the capital of the Eastern Frankish Empire. Soon the population outgrew the former Roman camp, and the city was extended for the first time around 900. Since it lay on the river, which formed the natural main traffic route, Regensburg expanded mainly along the Danube.

To the south-west, outside the walls of the fort, the monastery of St. Emmeram already existed, and so the new city wall was built around the monastery and then in a northerly direction, via today's Bismarckplatz and Arnulfsplatz and the Weißgerbergraben, to the Danube. The enclosed area had thus nearly doubled.

The city as a centre of political power with a large number of noblemen, clergy and gentlefolk was an important outlet for trade

and commerce, and the demand for luxury goods was huge. In addition to local manufacture, the import of goods of all kinds, from as far afield as the Orient, gained increasing significance. With respect to this long-distance trade, Regensburg had an advantage over many other cities through its central geographical situation. Most of the increasingly wealthy merchants' families settled in the newly enclosed area of the city. Jewish as well as Christian traders played an important part from early on. From the location of the Jewish ghetto, on the fringes of the city yet inside the Roman town walls (in the Neupfarrplatz

The Romanesque Allerheiligenkapelle (All Saints' Chapel) in the cathedral cloisters

area), it is possible to deduce that the ghetto must already have existed at an early stage, before the first extension of the city. When the Carolingian line died out in 911, Regensburg remained the residence of emperors and kings, and in addition Bavarian dukes resided here again from the mid-10th century onwards. The bishops sought to strengthen their power and the recently emerged class of rich patrician traders gained ever greater influence. All these groups together influenced the appearance of the city and built not only one, but several centres of power in the new Romanesque style.

The old palace precinct in Kornmarkt, which includes the Ducal Palace and the Römerturm (or Heidenturm), was altered and enlarged. The Bavarian duke Henry IV, later to become Emperor Henry II (1002 – 24), had the palace church, the Alte Kapelle (Old Chapel), extended. In the cathedral precinct, a Romanesque cathedral and baptistry were built, as well as the Allerheiligenkapelle (All Saints' Chapel), which was a burial chapel for Bishop Hartwig II (mid 12th century), and the Church of St Ulrich (first half of the

13th century). New monasteries were founded and old ones renovated (St Emmeram's, Niedermünster, Obermünster, Schotten-
kloster, Prüfening, Karthaus-Prüll). Bishops from other dioceses established courts to use during meetings of spiritual and temporal
dignitaries. The wealthy merchants began to build their castle-like
mansions with towers, the so-called 'patrician towers', in the Italian style.

The greatest achievement in the area of secular architecture
was undoubtedly the construction of the Steinerne Brücke (Stone
Bridge, 1135 – 146) over the Danube, a project which was vital both
for government and trade.

All these new buildings, of course, had to be decorated and furnished, and Regensburg is fortunate in that many works of art
and other features have remained in place. The porch of the monastery of St Emmeram contains the earliest large sculptures in Bavaria, Christ, Emmeram and Dionysius (1049). Inside the monastery church, in the graceful crypt of St Wolfgang, are the earliest
decorated cubiform capitals. Two very finely worked Romanesque
door-knockers in the form of lions' heads are still to be found on
the inner doors of Niedermünster (Lower Minster Church). Strange
mystical figures and ornaments from the late-12th century decorate the portal of the Schottenkirche (Scots' Church). Unique frescoes have been preserved in the Allerheiligenkapelle (c. 1180) and
the monastery church at Prüfening.

Besides the great works of art, many everyday objects such as
earthenware crockery and glass dating from the Romanesque
period form part of the collections in the local museums.

The Heyday and Decline of the Free Imperial City

A third group profited from the struggle for power between the
emperors and the church – the citizens of Regensburg. The im-
mensely rich merchants (several of whom had fortunes on a par
with those of the Fuggers, who later became so famous for their
wealth) had in the course of time already purchased many rights.
The decree issued by Emperor Frederick II in 1245 allowing the
city to elect its own mayor and govern itself marked the final step
towards achieving its sovereign status.

The splendour, however, was not of long duration. The small
area of the free imperial city was surrounded by Bavarian and

episcopal territory and thus was affected by decisions made by these powers. The Bavarian dukes in particular did all they could to force the wealthy merchant city to its knees, from founding towns nearby to erecting drastic trade barriers by way of taxes. The trade routes changed; other cities, for instance Nuremberg or Augsburg, which beside engaging in trade specialised in the manufacture of high quality products, became serious competitors. At the end of the 15th century Regensburg was already in such a hopeless financial state that the free imperial city voluntarily gave itself up to the Bavarian duke. The emperor however forced the duke to return the city a few years later so as to have it in his sphere of influence again.

When, however, Regensburg first became a free imperial city, several important building projects had to be completed. The city needed a new seat of government, a town hall. In the district of the merchants, close to the market square, a four-sided building with a tall awe-inspiring tower was erected, after the fashion of the great merchants' houses, next to it another building was constructed housing a magnificent hall above gloomy dungeons. The bishop, deprived of his power, decided to build a huge Gothic cathedral modelled on French examples. As the first and most important church of the city, it was also set on a pediment so that it

The Free Imperial City's Town Hall

dominated the city. New monasteries were also built, for instance those of the Minorites or Dominicans. There was hardly a single order which was not represented in Regensburg and the number of patrician towers grew with every new patrician mansion that was constructed. The flourishing city had once more expanded towards the Danube, the second extension of the city wall taking place not only in a westerly, but also in an easterly direction.

The architects, sculptors, painters and art craftsmen of the time still remained to a great extent, anonymous. Occasionally their Christian names were given or they were described by epithets. The 'Erminold Master' is an example. He was named after the tomb of the Blessed Erminold in the monastery at Prüfening which was created by him. Architect and sculptor at the same time, he had a significant influence on the construction of the cathedral: amongst other things he created the cathedral's most famous sculpture, the Smiling Angel, which is part of the Annunciation Group. The city's appearance is, to the present day, dominated by Gothic architecture. However, many buildings have not survived because this style was appreciated, but because there was no money for new, 'modern' buildings in later times. Not only Gothic buildings have been preserved, though, but also many furnishings and fittings which bear witness to the former greatness of the city: stained glass windows, sculptures, tapestries, paintings, objets d'art created by goldsmiths as well as many everyday artefacts. Regensburg was a poor city when

The tombstone of the Blessed Erminold in the church of St Georg at Prüfening

The tapestry depicting barbarians which used to hang in the Imperial Hall

the Renaissance heralded the beginning of modern times, and since, as was usual at that time, only the Jews were allowed to lend money, many citizens were deeply in debt to them. The Jews were then made scapegoats for the decline. They were expelled from the city by a resolution of the city council in 1519 and the ghetto was destroyed.

While the synagogue was being demolished, a worker fell off the scaffolding and lay as if dead; however he then stood up and walked home. This happy outcome to the accident was declared to be a 'miracle'. Thousands of pilgrims flocked to the city, bringing large amounts of money with them. The citizens began to build a huge pilgrimage church (a wooden model of which is on display at the Historical Museum, p. 81). However, the plague put an end to the pilgrimage after just a few years and the church remained incomplete. Fitted with a second choir, this edifice was later to become the 'Neue Pfarre', the city's first Protestant parish church, when it converted to the Protestant faith in 1542.

Ironically it was at this time of relative poverty, during which, apart from the construction of a few functional buildings, the only building activity was the alteration of some of the courtyards to include arcades, that Regensburg produced its greatest painter: Albrecht Altdorfer (about 1480 – 1538), the master of the Danube School. He created his exceptional works for such illustrious clients as the emperor, dukes, bishops and mon-asteries. With the exception of some prints, few of them have been preserved in Regensburg: the painting of the two Johns and a few fragments of the frescoes which decorated the bath chamber of the episcopal administrator, all now on display at the Historical Museum (p. 81), and a painting known as the Beautiful Mary in the Diocesan Museum (p. 82). Altdorfer became very famous and wealthy. He owned two properties in the city, was a member of the Inner Council and the city's master builder.

Bathing scene by Albrecht Altdorfer from the Bischofshof

The City of the Perpetual Imperial Diet (1663 – 1806)

The Thirty Years' War (1618 – 1648) did not leave Regensburg un-
scathed. In 1631 the city was occupied by Catholic troops loyal to
the emperor. For strategic reasons they destroyed a number of
suburbs and blasted one arch of the Steinerne Brücke. In 1633 the
city fell into the hands of the Protestant Swedish troops, only to
be recaptured by the emperor's troops the following year. The
chaos of war took its toll on Regensburg's population, and when
an epidemic of the plague broke out as well, the population was
reduced by about a fifth.

It was not until a quarter of a century after the Peace of West-
phalia that new splendour came to the city. The Perpetual Diet,
which was in its way the first German parliament, met in Regensburg from this time on. Not only the potentates of the Holy Roman Empire came together here; many foreign envoys also resided
inside the mediaeval walls as observers of the political proceed-
ings. In economic terms, this did not do much to help the city.
The guests paid no taxes, were allowed to import their goods free
of customs charges and, in addition, to employ their own artists
and craftsmen – much to the disadvantage of the local ones. Few
new buildings were erected, but others were restored, amongst
them two ancient churches which were splendidly redecorated in
the late Baroque or Rococo style: the Alte Kapelle and the monastery church of St Emmeram.

**The ballroom of the free imperial city at the Old Town Hall, which was
used as an assembly hall for the Imperial Diet**

The Century of Slumber (19th century)

The end of the empire and the loss of its status as a free imperial city brought Regensburg only a brief interlude as an independent political body. Prince-primate Carl von Dalberg ruled here for a few years, but then, in 1810, he gave up Regensburg – the Grand Duchy of Frankfurt had been created especially for him – and handed the city over to the Kingdom of Bavaria. Innumerable precious works of art were taken to Munich at that time. Regensburg became a sleepy provincial town, which it remained until well into the 20th century. The absence of industry also meant little wealth, little chance to change anything – thank goodness, we might say today with hindsight.

Regensburg Awakens

At the beginning of the 20th century Regensburg was still described as an old and ugly city; but since World War II, during which Regensburg suffered very little damage, much has been done to enhance and enliven the city. New industry, the university and the polytechnic have given it a more dynamic atmosphere, and the unceasing efforts to restore and conserve the historical fabric, coupled with a growing awareness of the city's great heritage, have made it more beautiful than ever.

The university, which lies in the south of the city

Conservation and World Heritage

In Regensburg, too, projects were mooted which, in hindsight, would have done immeasurable harm to the ancient city centre. For instance, a four-lane road parallel to the Danube was planned in order to create, as was considered desirable in the 1960s, a more traffic-friendly city. However, Regensburg was always fortunate to have sufficient committed citizens who, realising the uniqueness of what had been preserved, banded together to fight against its planned destruction and did their best to support the two conservation offices in the city – the municipal one and the Bavarian one – in their often desperate efforts to convince the authorities that they were making mistakes. It must be admitted that the protesters, too, were not always successful. Despite that, Regensburg today is the best preserved mediaeval city with the largest number of Romanesque and Gothic architectural monuments north of the Alps. The development of the city is not only confined to the Middle Ages, however. It begins much earlier with the Roman military camp and the adjoining civilian settlement, with the arrival of the Baiuvarii, the ancient Bavarians, with the city's growth beyond the limits of the Roman camp (Germany's earliest large-scale urban extension) in about 900. Then, after a second period of expansion about 1300 and after some centuries of stagnation, Regensburg experienced another period of dramatic growth in the 19th century and, above all, in the 20th century. And this expansion is still continuing. Thus it is possible to speak of a continuous, and what is more, of an ever faster process of urban development, which augurs well for the future.

What is more, the old town centre offers evidence of cultural and political traditions that tells us of events in Regensburg in past centuries: court assemblies in the days of the Agilolfing dukes, imperial diets during the Holy Roman Empire, the Perpetual Imperial Diet – all these can be associated with particular historical locations.

Regensburg has also managed to prevent its great heritage becoming a 'museum-like island'; the ancient centre is still a truly multi-functional area, in which its various functions continue to enjoy equal status. Thanks to the local regulations for the preservation of the old city centre and the Bavarian act governing the conservation of ancient monuments, both dating from 1973 and both not only uttering prohibitions but also offering assistance in dealing with historic buildings, the old city centre has developed, if not into an 'island of bliss', then at least into an urban area which it is a real pleasure to live in. The research into and documentation of all the city-centre buildings are exemplary; from 1973 on, architectural histories of all the buildings in the old town have appeared at regular intervals in separate volumes for each of its various districts, and 984 of these buildings have now been added to UNESCO's World Heritage List. The city authorities have now set up a database encompassing all the city's historic buildings, so that one can go on a virtual tour of the Old Town, Stadtamhof and parts of the Danube islands, which together make up World Heritage Regensburg: www.regensburg.de/welterbe/denkmal_db.

Why the City of the Imperial Diets is Home for the House of Thurn and Taxis

The emperors convened their imperial assemblies at Regensburg time and again. Though the exact figure is not known, at least 60 assemblies took place here. The three estates of the empire – the prince electors, the princes and the free imperial cities – usually came together in the free imperial city's town hall. The opening and closing assemblies took place in the magnificent Reichssaal (Imperial Hall). The order of the seating was arranged carefully according to rank. The emperor sat enthroned at the front of the room on a dais with four steps, the prince electors were on either side of him, but raised only two steps above the room.

The Prince-Electors' room at the Old Town Hall

The princes, who sat on benches running the length of the room, had the right to one step. The representatives of the imperial cities were relegated to the back part of the room and sat at ground level. The meeting rooms of the estates were also symbolic of their importance. The prince electors, being the most important body, had the best rooms – those of the Inner Council – in spite of their small number, which varied between six and eight. The princes, the largest group, which had about a hundred members, had only a relatively small room next to the Reichssaal, while the imperial cities, of which there were fifty-one, were allocated in rooms under the roof.

As the imperial diets usually only lasted for a few weeks or months, the city enjoyed acting as their host. The pomp and splendour which was displayed at the many festivities during the imperial assemblies offered excellent entertainment for Regensburg's citizens as well. After the Perpetual Diet had been established in Regensburg in 1663, the city decided to hand over its 'old' town hall to the Diet completely. A new town hall was built right next door – today an even newer one stands in Minoritenweg. The princes were assigned one additional room, otherwise the distribution of the meeting chambers remained as before. Because the emperors were not constantly present at the Perpetual Diet, the post of the Imperial Principal Commissioner was created. As the representative of the monarch, he had to be a member of the highest aristocracy. In addition, it was desirable that he should possess a sizeable personal fortune, because he himself had to pay for most of the festivities which he organized in the emperor's name and in his sovereign's honour. In 1748 Prince Alexander Ferdinand von Thurn und Taxis was made Imperial Principal Commissioner. From then on until the end of the empire in 1806, this office remained in the hands of his family. The members of this bourgeois merchant family had made a fortune by organising a regular postal service. For hundreds of years the Thurn and Taxis family held the postal monopoly for the whole of the

A Proverbial German Saying...

... originated at the Perpetual Diet:
'To make a decision at the green table'
meaning 'to make a decision of little practical relevance': the table in the prince electors' chamber was covered with green baize. Here many decisions were taken which turned out to be unworldly and far removed from the every-day worries of the people outside.

The Palace of the Princes of Thurn and Taxis

empire. From Frankfurt, where it had resided since 1702, the princely family moved to Regensburg. Since the princes were not citizens of the free imperial city, they were, however, not allowed to buy property inside the city walls. Just like all the other members of the imperial diet, they had to rent accommodation. It was not until the city's imperial freedom ended that the princely family was able to purchase and move into a residence, consisting of the buildings of the dissolved monastery of St Emmeram. The princely family has remained in Regensburg to the present day and still contributes a lot to the city's fame.

Regensburg from Side to Side and Back Again, or from Top to Bottom

Three Walks through the City

The various routes are marked on the plan (inside front cover) of the city, the various monuments are numbered in the text as well as on the map. For visitors who do not have much time, the most important monuments are marked with three asterisks (*): what you simply must see; two asterisks: what you really ought to see; and one asterisk: what's also worth seeing.

Route A

From the Suburbs to the Suburbs – from the Station to Stadtamhof

Via Regensburg's green belt to the former monastery of St Emmeram, from there through the Bachgasse to the Goldener Turm, past Don Juan to Fischmarkt and the former Danube port, over the Steinerne Brücke and the Wöhrd Islands to Stadtamhof. (Town plan inside front cover)

In 1859 the railway reached Regensburg. The route from Nuremberg to Munich ran along the southern fringe of the historic city centre and caused an expansion of the city to the south for the first time since Roman days. The visitor is welcomed by the **ring of avenues (1)** which surrounds the city today in place of the medieval city fortifications. As we leave the station we immediately see the first of the city's many churches, the little Church of St Peter, which originally lay in the middle of a Catholic cemetery. The Protestant cemetery adjoined it on the city side. The famous astronomer and mathematician **Johannes Kepler** was laid to rest here in 1630, though only for a short time. Just three years later, during the Thirty Years' War, his grave was destroyed. In 1808 Regensburg citizens erect-

Fürst-Anselm-Allee, one of the avenues that form part of the green belt around Regensburg

The Kepler Memorial

ed in his honour a small Grecian rotunda containing his bust in the park on the opposite side of Maximilianstraße.

The **statue of King Ludwig I on horseback (2)** originally stood in the cathedral square, but soon had to make way for the traffic and was moved to its present location. It is to Ludwig I that Regensburg owes the completion of its Gothic cathedral, as well as the Walhalla and the Befreiungshalle (Hall of Liberation) in the surrounding region. There is a good chance that, when the cathedral square is refurbished, the equestrian statue will return to the site it was created for. **Maximilianstraße**, one of the city's widest streets, which leads in a straight line from the station into the heart of the city, is a result of Napoleon's campaigns. During the battle in 1809 against the Austrians, who were approaching from the north, his troops set fire to the whole southern area of the city with its narrow, crooked alleys.

Only a few yards to the right of the approach to the historic city centre, some huge stone blocks rise from the ground. They formed the south-eastern corner of **Castra Regina (3)**, the Roman military fort. These walls, which were constructed more than 1800 years ago, have survived the centuries and were also reinforced by mediaeval fortifications.

Recrossing Maximilianstraße and continuing along St.-Petersweg, past the massive neo-Rococo complex of the Parkhotel (1890), we can, just before reaching the last house on this side of the road, peer down into a garden that was laid out in the city's mediaeval moat. Immediately afterwards, Fröhliche-Türken-Straße leads into the centre of town. This was the site of St Peter's Gate,

Regensburg Street Names

In Regensburg one encounters a number of strange street names, which seem to be taken from the world of creatures and plants: blue, white and red lilies, golden and black bears, white and red cocks, ducks, doves, a white lamb and a silver fish, a cow, a crab and a dog. It was almost always taverns which gave their names to the streets they stood in. This was what also happened in Fröhliche-Türken-Straße (Jolly Turk Road), where a pub called 'The Jolly Man' was situated. Its owners were called Türk, and in the course of time, the 'Jolly Man' became the 'Jolly Turk'.

where one used to enter the city from the south before Maximil-ianstraße existed.

St.-Petersweg continues past the Thurn and Taxis park, the only part of the green belt not open to the public, and then, just before the Thurn and Taxis palace comes into view on the left, a small curving road (An der Hülling) forks off to the right, indicating the course of the Roman town wall, i.e. this was the south-western corner of the fort.

A bit further on, we reach **Emmeramsplatz**. To the north and east it is enclosed by impressive Classicist buildings, which are to-day occupied by the government of the Oberpfalz; to the south, however, one of the greatest gems of the city lies hidden, the former *****Benedictine monastery of St Emmeram (4)**, one of the most ancient foundations in the whole of Bavaria.

In the course of its long history and because of several fires, it was rebuilt and altered again and again, so that today it is com-posed of superb elements of almost every style and epoch. Through a double portal set in a Gothic wall (c. 1250) we enter the elongated forecourt, containing graves from various centuries (the first on the right is that of Aventinus, Bavaria's earliest historian).

To the left is the bell tower, which was altered during the Re-naissance and stands apart from the church after the Italian fash-ion. From the massive, slightly sunken Romanesque vestibule, a door on the left leads to the monastery's former parish church of St Rupert (14th to 18th cent.), while two portals beside it lead di-rectly into the monastery church. Next to and above the two door recesses there are three figures: Christ, with a portrayal of the founder at his feet, is flanked by the monastery's patron St Em-meram (to the left) and St Dionysius (to the right). There is a spe-cial reason why St Dionysius (St Dennis) is portrayed here. It seemed advantageous to own valuable relics to further the monas-tery's aim of becoming directly subject to the emperor. Thus it was simply claimed that the monastery possessed relics of St Di-onysius, and the statue was set up as proof of this.

The two doors lead into different areas of the church, and through the right-hand one we enter the impressive, dark Roman-esque west transept (mid 11th century) with its raised choir and its painted Baroque coffered wooden ceiling. Below the choir is the crypt of St Wolfgang, which surprisingly enough for its time of construction (it was consecrated in 1052) is not bulky and heavy in style, but amazingly light and elegant.

The 19th-century shrine in the altar contains the relics of St Wolfgang, who is possibly better known from the Austrian lake named after him than because of his time as a bishop of Regensburg. Until his period of office, the bishop of Regensburg was at the same time abbot of St Emmeram. Wolfgang separated the two offices. In spite of this he was buried here like his predecessors.

If we enter the church by the left door or step through the grille separating the main part of the church from the west transept, we enter a completely different kind of room. The whole wealth of the famous abbey is reflected in the nave, which was magnificently redecorated in the late Baroque period (1731–1733). The huge ceiling painting illustrates the martyrdom of Roman Christians on this spot while along the richly decorated walls of the nave, painted scenes from the legend of St Emmeram alternate with statues of famous people who either originally came from the monastery, such as William of Hirsau, or were closely connected with it, such as Charlemagne.

St Emmeram had served as a preacher and father confessor at the court of the Agilolfing dukes. After the unmarried daughter of a duke had confided to him that she was pregnant and he had claimed to be the child's father so as to protect her, the girl's enraged brother murdered him south of Munich while he was on a journey to Rome. The transfer of the saint's remains back to Regensburg caused pilgrims to flock to Regensburg for many centuries.

The artists who executed most of the paintings and stucco work in St Emmeram were the brothers Cosmas Damian

The monk in St Emmeram's

(1686 – 1739) and Egid Quirin (1692 – 1750) Asam, who, as was their habit, included one humorous detail: at that time the building operations were under the constant supervision of a strict monk. While he had gone away on a short journey, the Asams created a likeness of him and placed it in the round window on the top right-hand side, next to the organ.

Hemma, consort of Ludwig the German

The epitaphs of many personages of high rank decorate the interior of the church. At the entrance to the left side choir, the elegant Gothic tomb stone (c. 1280) of Queen Hemma, wife of Ludwig the German, is set in the wall. Then come the tombs of Henry the Quarrelsome (c. 1330), Arnulf of Bavaria (12th cent.) and the Blessed Aurelia (c. 1330). According to legend, the daughter of the Kapetings lived near the monastery as an anchorite in the 11th century. It is possible to imagine what the monastery church used to look like by looking at the south wall of this side choir. Romanesque decorative arches have been uncovered as well as Roman blocks of stone, which were reused here, as was common practice in Romanesque buildings. From here a flight of steps leads down to the church's second crypt, that of St Emmeram. As a so-called circular crypt it leads around the main choir and one re-enters the main church from the southern side choir right by the tomb of the patron saint. The names of the first bishops of Regensburg are inscribed on paving flags down the church's southern aisle. St Wolfgang's grave is protected by a mediaeval grille.

Today St Emmeram is a parish church, but it is also the family church of the Thurn and Taxis family. For instance, the late Prince Johannes and Princess Mariae Gloria were married here in 1980 and, on leaving the church through one of the portals, one sees a narrow passage that leads directly from the porch onto the road to the palace. The former monastery buildings came into the ownership of the Thurn and Taxis family after the secularisation of 1812. After alterations and extensions in the 19th century, they were turned into the **Fürstliches Schloss (5)** (Palace of the Princes of Thurn and Taxis), which is said to have more rooms than Buckingham Palace.

The monastery's ancient cloisters including the burial chapel of the princely family and the palace's staterooms can be visited in the course of a guided tour. The Marstall (Stable Block), which houses a splendid collection of carriages (but only private ones, there is not a single mail coach), also merits a visit, as well as the collection of silver and gold valuables which the princely family made over to the Bavarian state after the death of Prince Johannes in return for the waiving of inheritance tax. The two glass buildings which enclose the forecourt of the stables (c. 1830) were built in connection with the major anniversary exhibition entitled '500 Years of Postal Services' in 1990; one of them is used as a ticket office and entrance to the museum, the second is the 'Café Gloria', as it is popularly known.

After returning to Emmeramsplatz, if we turn right and walk past the Protestant Hospital, which is on the left-hand side, we come to **Obere Bachgasse**. Until the 19th century a stream called the Vitusbach (which has since been rerouted as a subterranean canal) flowed along the middle of this street, which is the longest in the historic city centre. It served not only as an easy means of transport for goods, but also for the disposal of waste, which was discharged directly into the Danube. Houses dating from various centuries line the road. First come

Ballroom in the Palace of the Princes of Thurn and Taxis

Obere Bachgasse facing south, showing the house once belonging to the Altdorfer family

the mediaeval former outbuildings of the Obermünster Convent, which was destroyed during World War II (today, they house the Diocesan Museum, where special exhibitions take place), adjoining them is a house decorated with murals dating from the 1920s. On the corner of Blaue-Sterngasse the sumptuously decorated Romanesque portal of a private chapel (c. 1200) has been preserved. The house on the corner of Augustinergasse, with a statue of the Virgin set into its facade at first floor-level, was at one time inhabited by **Albrecht Altdorfer (6)**, the city's most famous painter. At that time, though, the house looked very different. The roof was added to the massive tower later and, at the same time, the house was redecorated in the Baroque style. The little bakery on the ground-floor of the tower, once owned by a family called Schwarzer, is famous throughout Regensburg for its bread rolls. The 'Schwarzer Kipferl', oval rye rolls spiced with caraway, which are freshly baked several times a day, are one of the city's specialities and are served in the city's beergardens, along with 'Weichser Radi', a type of white radish, the sweetish mustard produced by the Händlmaier factory and 'Knacker', a small, fat type of sausage that is known as 'Regensburger' elsewhere. By crossing the Gesandtenstraße (Route C, p. 56), we reach the part of town containing most of the houses built by merchant families that had grown wealthy through long-distance trade. In imitation of Italian models, these were castle-like houses with towers. These towers symbolised wealth, the higher the tower, the richer the family (even if this was not always quite true). These 'mediaeval skyscrapers' were up to twelve storeys high, at one time 60 of them existed in the city. More than twenty of them have survived, though they are usually not preserved in their full height.

The highest residential tower, the ***Goldener Turm (7)** (Golden Tower, 2nd half of the 13th century), which can be seen from the courtyard of Untere Bachgasse No 7 and from Wahlenstraße, actually still has nine stories. Originally the towers were only inhabited to the level of the top floors of the houses. Above, there were either store-rooms or stairs leading to the very top. Today, it is regarded as particularly fashionable to live in these towers. The house to which the Goldener Turm belonged was a typical merchant's house with broad gateways, a courtyard from which stairs led to the cellars and a gable door through which goods could be winched up into the loft. Today it is a students' residence, and it is due to this fact that the courtyard is today open to the public. In the Middle Ages courtyards served exclusively for private and commercial purposes. As we leave the courtyard through the gate opposite leading to Wahlenstraße, we can still see the vaulting of the private chapel in the shop on the left. Quite a few of the merchants' houses had their own private chapels. They were all deprived of both their function and their furnishings, however, when the

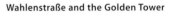

Wahlenstraße and the Golden Tower

free imperial city converted to the Protestant faith in 1542 and all the citizens had to become Protestants. Nevertheless, the ecclesiastical architecture has remained in many cases, as can be seen by peering into various shop windows in the city. If we turn left along Wahlenstraße, we reach **Kohlenmarkt (8)** (The Coal Market), the first of the early medieval city's market squares. It lay outside the walls of the Roman fort, which ran between Bachgasse and Wahlenstraße and turned right at the edge of the square (northwestern corner of the fort). The fountain and trees were added just a few years ago, and in summer the square's cafés are popular meeting places. At this point we cross Route B (p. 42).

Don Juan de Austria, hero of the naval battle of Lepanto

On the far side another, smaller square, Zieroldsplatz, opens off Kohlenmarkt. Here stands the Baroque statue of **Don Juan de Austria** (Don John of Austria, p. 54). It is a copy of the monument that was erected in Messina to commemorate his victory in the naval battle of Lepanto. Straight on from here lies **Fischmarkt (9)** (The Fish Market), where until a few years ago fish from the rivers and lakes in the vicinity was sold on the old stone benches every Friday. From the fountain in Fischmarkt water can be drawn as required by pulling the water spouts downwards.

From here we should take a small detour to the left into **Keplerstraße**. In this street, which runs parallel to the Danube, important merchants built

View of the Amberg Salt Store from Fischmarkt

their houses so as to be as near as possible to the hub of economic activity, the port. The street was renamed Keplerstraße only about a hundred years ago, because the great astronomer lived here for a time with his family and also died here. The house in which he lived, on the corner of 'Am Schallern', was refurbished a few years ago and the decorative old murals were restored. On the way to the house in which Kepler died (No 5), we pass the mighty Gothic *Runtingerhaus (10)* (No 1, c. 1200 – 1400) . The Runtinger family was incredibly wealthy, but only for two generations. For many years the family presided over the house of the German merchants' guild in Venice, the Fondaco dei Tedeschi. There the Runtingers bought 2000 bull's-eye window panes, which cost a fortune in those days. This piece of information is gleaned from the family's account books of c. 1400, which are documents invaluable to historians of mediaeval trade. As the panes were not resold, it is reasonable to assume that they were the ones used to glaze the windows of the Runtingers' magnificent private ballroom. More than 200 square metres in area, this is one of the largest and most beautiful halls in the city and, like other similar rooms, it is used for various cultural events today.

The Runtingerhaus with its ballroom on the first floor

Two houses further along is the **Kepler Memorial Museum (11)** (No 5, altered to its present-day form in 1540, p. 82). Kepler stayed with a friend in this house when he came to Regensburg after Wallenstein, his employer, had been deposed in 1630. He planned to demand his outstanding salary from the emperor, who was holding an imperial diet here. But before he was granted an audience, Kepler died from a sudden serious illness.

On the way back to Fischmarkt, the **Weinstadel** (Wine Store, No 14) stands on the left-hand side, a massive building, presumably constructed according to a design by the city's master-builder of the time, Albrecht Altdorfer. The city had (and still has) a long wine-growing tradition. Probably wine had been grown on the gentle slopes north of the Danube ever since Roman times. The harvest, however, was not sufficient by far and therefore year after year large shipments had to be transported along the Danube from Ulm in Württemberg to Regensburg. Wine was the drink of the wealthy, the poor drank beer.

The little house next door, which juts out far into the street, bears the name '**Zum Sauseneck**', because the Vitusbach (p. 29), which had a strong current, noisily gushed around the corner here. The mediaeval port of Regensburg was situated near **Am Wiedfang (12)**, to the north of Fischmarkt. The port basin was filled by the Danube, which entered it where one today sees a small section of the city wall. When the port later was moved down the Danube, the basin was filled in and built upon. The small houses along the city wall belonged to poorer people. The location directly behind the wall was extremely dangerous during enemy attack; however, these houses were cheap to erect as only three walls needed to be built.

If we go left through the city wall, we find ourselves directly on the riverbank below the ***Steinerne Brücke (13)** (Stone Bridge, 1135 – 1146), the masterpiece of Romanesque secular architecture. The importance of the bridge from the very beginning can be gathered from the fact that the office of 'Master of the Bridge' was created. The office-holder received the proceeds from several public bath houses for the upkeep of the bridge. A special seal was also created for the bridge; today it is used by Regensburg University. Even in prehistoric times there was a ford across the river here, at the time of Charlemagne a pontoon bridge spanned the Dan-

The Steinerne Brücke, looking towards Stadtamhof

ube, and this was followed by several wooden bridges in later times. These, however, had to be rebuilt from scratch every time the Danube flooded or froze, causing ice floes to pile up against the bridge. In a concerted effort, the duke and the bishop, probably with financial support from the rich merchants, constructed a bridge of stone that measured 330 m in length and originally had 16 arches (the one nearest the city has since been built over), a magnificent feat of engineering for those days. The massive piers of the bridge were built over frames made of oak beams and to protect the piers from damage by water or ice, boat-shaped bases were built around them. Though these were good for the bridge's stability, they made shipping much more difficult. Because of their width the space for the water to pass through is reduced by two-thirds and the current is, in consequence, much stronger around the bridge. Up to the middle of the 17th century, numerous mills stood on the bases of the pillars and made use of the energy generated by the water. However, ships could only be towed upstream under the bridge with the aid of a powerful winch. This winch was anchored in the small building with the wide wooden flap just beside the passage on the right-hand side. As a result of the completion of the canal to the north of the Danube (1973), only tourist boats and leisure craft now pass under the bridge.

After the Steinerne Brücke, where the Danube once more fills the whole width of the river bed, the famous Strudel forms the ever-changing eddies which have been the subject of many songs and poems. The bridge has also changed in the course of the centuries. As a permanently open entrance to the city, it had to be fortified. Three towers (only the one on the city side has survived) were constructed as well as a bastion at its northern end. Much has been lost of the bridge's original decorations, although the **Bruckmandl**, the 'little man on the bridge', has been preserved at the bridge's highest point.

The Legend of the 'Bruckmandl'

According to legend, this little man is the bridge's master-builder. He sits on a pointed stone and looks towards the cathedral, shading his eyes with his hand. This is because he is said to have made a bet with the cathedral's architect as to who would finish his work sooner. As he was delayed in completing the bridge, he asked the devil to help him. The devil was happy to assist, but as a reward he demanded the souls of first three living creatures to cross the bridge. Of course the bridge was finished first and when the duke, the bishop and the city's wealthy merchants came to view this marvel of architecture, the master-builder was in great distress. But then he had an ingenious idea: he chased a dog, a cock and a hen across the bridge. The devil saw that he was being cheated out of his reward and, in his rage, attempted to destroy the bridge. He stooped down under the middle arch and tried to shove it upwards with his back and break it. Though he did not quite succeed, the bridge has had a slight hump in the middle ever since.

The **Historische Wurstküche** (Historic Sausage Kitchen), a small building that is at least 500 years old, is a traditional meeting place for those who enjoy eating little grilled sausages and sauerkraut. Next to it stands the impressive seven-storey ****Salzstadel (14)** (Salt Store) with its steep roof. It was built in 1620 as the city's biggest salt store and was restored at a cost of several million euros in 1986 – 1989.

At the end of the building facing the Wurstküche, the door on the left leads to the ground floor, which is solidly constructed of stone and wood, while the other storeys are constructed only of wood, using huge oak beams. Regensburg held the monopoly for trading in salt for the whole of the Oberpfalz. And salt was regarded as 'white gold'. An illustration on the first floor shows the difficult route that this vital commodity had to take to reach Regensburg. From the saltworks in Reichenhall it was transported to Passau, partly by land, partly on rafts down the river Inn.

The 'Historische Wurstküche', meeting-place of all sausage-lovers

There it was loaded onto ships which were connected up to form a 'salt train', which was pulled upstream against the current by teams of three to four dozen horses. A shipment of this type took about a fortnight. In Regensburg the salt was stored and sold gradually. The fact that the stone and the woodwork of the Salzstadel have become permeated by salt poses almost insoluble problems as regards the present-day use of the huge building. As no paper can be kept here because of the salt contamination, plans to house the city library or archives in the building had to be abandoned. Finding a use for the **Amberger Salzstadel** on the other side of the bridge ramp was much less of a problem: after it had been restored students moved into the building.

The **Brückturm** (Bridge Tower) with its narrow arch provided the only access to the bridge until the beginning of the 20th century. It was not until 1902 that three small houses were demolished to permit the construction of a broader ramp up to the bridge, which is spanned by an arch. This alteration became necessary because of the electric tram which crossed the bridge in those days. The Bridge, closed to traffic since 1997, is now reserved for pedestrians. The bridge's first two arches were blasted by the National

Socialists in the closing days of World War II, when American soldiers had already advanced very near, and it was not until 1967 that the bridge was repaired. Looking back towards the tower as we cross the bridge, we see the statues of King Philipp, his wife Irene and Emperor Frederick II set high up on the wall of the tower (the originals are in the Historical Museum, p. 81). They were originally affixed to the two gate towers which have been destroyed and showed the traveller that he was entering a free imperial city. It was these two monarchs who granted Regensburg the necessary privileges.

An old Regensburg Saying

An old saying asserts that unless you have crossed the Stone Bridge, met a Jew and heard the church bells ringing, you have not been to Regensburg.

Villa Lauser, once the summer residence of the Thon-Dittmer family

The two Wöhrd Islands (the name derives from a German word meaning a steep bank) to the right and left of the bridge are popular with Regensburg's inhabitants for walks, a visit to the beer garden there or a picnic under the tall, shady trees. These trees have not been harmed by being immersed in water repeatedly during floods. From the Upper Wöhrd to the left of the bridge, where Regensburg fishermen and bargemen used to live and where rich tradesmen later built their summer villas (for instance Villa Lauser, No 2 Lieblstraße), we have a wonderful view of the historic city centre.

While the Wöhrd Islands were always part of the free imperial city, 'enemy territory' began north of the bridge: **Stadtamhof** was Bavarian. Only the fortified bridgehead, which was demolished in 1810 after it had been badly damaged by Austrian troops (p. 40), and **St Katharine's Hospital (15)** immediately to the left of it be–longed to Regensburg. The hospital was moved to this location from the cathedral precinct after the Steinerne Brücke was built. In its early days it was a kind of hospital for the poor. Later it was turned into an old people's home for needy citizens, a function it still has today. Its history was extremely turbulent. It was founded by Bishop Konrad at the beginning of the 13th century, destroyed several times, just like the rest of Stadtamhof, but rebuilt again and again. Besides the church and the building which housed the

Stadtamhof, facing south

wards, the hospital's brewery has also survived and the Hospital's beer garden is one of the most popular ones in the city (p. 88). Although Stadtamhof, which was made a market town as early as 1151, and a borough at the end of the 15th century, and then became part of Regensburg in 1924, profited from the trade route across the Steinerne Brücke, it was also the first place to suffer in the case of enemy attack. In every war the town was almost totally destroyed, first by Regensburg during the War of the Cities (1388), then during the Thirty Years' War, the Spanish Wars of Succession (1702) and finally during Napoleon's campaign against the Austrians (1809).

That is why most of the buildings, above all those which line the wide main street, which looks almost like a square, date from the 19th century, the time of the French Empire style. However, few of the facades are decorated with the lavishness that was fashionable at that period. Most of the townspeople no longer had sufficient means to do that when they rebuilt their houses – the only exception was the owner of the property Am Brückenfuß No 5. At the end of the main street stands a gateway consisting of two square pillars, beyond which the Main-Danube Canal flows. Since its completion in 1973, quite large cargo boats, too, can bypass the low, narrow Danube bridge. On the ridge beyond the canal, the Osterberg, stands the Church of the Holy Trinity, which the townspeople of Stadtamhof and Steinweg (the part of town which adjoins Stadtamhof to the north) vowed to build during the plague epidemic of 1713 and completed within a year.

Stadtamhof's main church is *St Mang (16)**. St Magnus, a monk from St Gallen, christianized the Allgäu in the 8th century and a church dedicated to him already existed in Stadtamhof in the 11th century. In 1138 an Augustinian canonical foundation was built next to it and attained great wealth and fame due to the many pilgrims that visited it. But here, too, the Thirty Years' War left its mark. The monastery and church were destroyed in 1633/34 and it was not until half a century later that the church was rebuilt.

The interior of the church displays magnificent Rococo decorations and its stucco-work in particular is reminiscent of St Emmeram's. Today, the monastery buildings house the Academy of Catholic Church Music and Musical Education.

By walking through the idyllic Wassergasse, across the Grieser Steg, the Lower Wöhrd and the modern Eiserne Brücke, we can reach the beginning of Route B (p. 42); alternatively, by recrossing the Steinerne Brücke and continuing along the Upper Wöhrd and across the Eiserner Steg and on along Weißgerbergraben, we come to Arnulfsplatz and the beginning of Route C (p. 56).

Effigy of St Michael above the pulpit in St Mang's Church

Route B

From East to West – following the Course of the Danube

*From the north-eastern corner of the Roman fort to the Porta Praetoria,
from the Bischofshof via Watmarkt past the Baumburgerturm to the
Old and the New Town Halls, from Haidplatz, the city's festival site, to
the Temple of the Muses. (Town plan inside front cover)*

**Lively market scene at the Donaumarkt
on a Saturday morning**

On a site where a large car park was created by pulling down various buildings after the Second World War (except on Saturday mornings, when the **Donaumarkt (17)** (Danube Market) lives up to its name because the weekly market is held here), traces of the city's Roman origins can be found. The massive stone blocks which can be seen on the south-western edge of the market place formed the north-eastern corner of **Castra Regina**, the Roman legionary fort, and are 1800 years old. However, they came to light again only when the houses that had been built in front of them were demolished at the beginning of our century.

The road along the former Roman wall is called **Unter den Schwibbögen** (Under the Flying Buttresses). Such buttresses do not stand on their own, but are squeezed in between two houses and often include walkways, as was originally the case here. Three of these arches linked houses on either side of the street up to the 19th century. The street contains a particularly imaginative sign outside the pub called '**Zum Walfisch**' ('The Whale', No 21), which

Jonah and the whale, the sign outside the Gasthof Zum Walfisch

shows Jonah jumping out of the mouth of a somewhat strangely shaped whale. A little coach shows that the mail coaches also stopped here. The pub was made particularly famous by the English ambassador to the Perpetual Diet, Sir George Etherege. The London bon-vivant found Regensburg too boring, so he engaged in an amorous adventure with an actress of doubtful reputation who lodged at the 'Whale'. This greatly enraged some youths, who demanded he surrender her to them in the name of law and order. Etherege, however, the perfect gentleman, defended the lady heroically.

A few steps further on, the gate house of the **Porta Praetoria (18)** (179 AD) juts out into the street on the left hand side. It is the

Model at the Historical Museum illustrating the construction of the Porta Praetoria

only original Roman building in Germany to have survived above ground level, apart from the Porta Nigra in Trier. Although only one arch is visible beside the tower, we know what the whole gateway looked like, because the Romans built all their gateways in identical fashion: two towers (the second is marked on the pavement) stood on either side of two gates. The left one was probably already blocked up in Roman times.

For those who wish to learn more about the Romans, a visit to the Historical Museum's Roman section is highly recommendable (p. 81); amongst other things it contains a model of the Porta Praetoria under construction which gives a detailed idea of the techniques used. After the former Via Praetoria, which used to run across the fort from north to south, had been blocked by the Romanesque cathedral, the gate became superfluous. It was built over and forgotten for centuries. Not until 1885 was it discovered by chance, when the brewery belonging at the Bischofshof was moved to a new site west of the city. Excavations were carried out and since then people have been able to marvel at the gateway, which also illustrates how much the level of the ground has 'risen' in the course of the centuries. While most of the base of the tower is below ground today, one has to climb another 14 steps to reach the interior of the fort, which was originally on a level with the gate. Through the gate one now enters the courtyard of the **Bischofshof (19)**, formerly the bishop's palace. The bishops took up residence here only after the offices of abbot of St Emmeram's and bishop of Regensburg were separated. The buildings standing here today are mainly Gothic and Renaissance. They were often used by the emperors when they stayed here during the imperial diets, and in 1810 Regensburg was formally incorporated into the kingdom of Bavaria here. Since then, the bishops have resided in the former convent of Niedermünster (p. 68) and the Bischofshof contains, besides the Cathedral Treasury Museum (p. 79), offices and business premises, a long-established hotel with a charming beergarden. From the latter, the whole height and length of the cathedral is visible (p. 64). The construction of this Gothic cathedral was begun in the second half of the 13th century. As it was to be foreseen that the building work would go on for a long time, the old Romanesque cathedral was not demolished all at once. The choir was left standing and continued to be used. For this reason the new building was sited further to the west. The new choir was erected where the old nave had stood. One of the towers in the facade of the old cathedral was also left. It was used during construction to hoist stones up to the level at which they were needed. Such a construction was called a 'donkey' in mediaeval times, and that is why the tower is popularly called the **'Donkey Tower'**. The intention was to encase it later, as remains of masonry on the left and right indicate. The modern fountain (by J. M. Neustifter, 1980) in the courtyard of the Bischofshof illustrates a mediaeval legend, the **Sermon to the Geese**. As was usual in the Middle Ages (see Haus Heuport, p. 63), this legend also conveys a message about the positive and negative aspects of human existence. St Francis of Assisi said that he expected his fellow friars to care for all living creatures, not just for human beings, and he himself set a good example by preaching to birds and fish. The priest shown here is preaching virtuously and with great conviction to a flock of geese, which gather around him trustingly. That, at least, is what it looks like from the front. Walking round behind the cleric, the observer spies a fox emerging from the folds of the man's cassock to seize the plumpest goose.

The 'Sermon to the Geese'

If we leave the courtyard through its western gate and cross the road, we reach one of those narrow alleys typical of the historic city centre; this one is in the area where the small traders known as 'Tändler' and 'Krämer', after whom nearby alleys are named, had their shops. This alley is called **Watmarkt**. The name, deriving from the mediaeval word 'wat' meaning clothes, shows that the cloth market took place here.

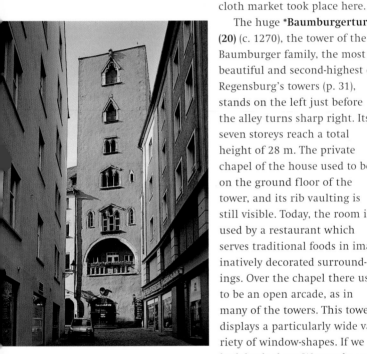

The tower-like mansion of the Baum-burger family in Watmarkt

The huge ***Baumburgerturm (20)** (c. 1270), the tower of the Baumburger family, the most beautiful and second-highest of Regensburg's towers (p. 31), stands on the left just before the alley turns sharp right. Its seven storeys reach a total height of 28 m. The private chapel of the house used to be on the ground floor of the tower, and its rib vaulting is still visible. Today, the room is used by a restaurant which serves traditional foods in imaginatively decorated surroundings. Over the chapel there used to be an open arcade, as in many of the towers. This tower displays a particularly wide variety of window-shapes. If we look back along Watmarkt, we can see another two of the city's many towers. In Goliathstraße it is well worth making a short detour to the right. If we cross the road and walk the short distance to Brückstraße, we have a good view of the Brückturm (p. 37) on the one hand, and of the painted facade of the ***Goliathhaus (21)** (13th to 16th century) on the other. Towards the end of the 16th century, painted facades such as this one, showing scenes from Greek or Roman history or the Bible, were fashionable.

David and Goliath – larger than lifesize on the wall of the Goliathhaus

But this is the only instance in which this type of facade decoration has been preserved, and even here the fresco has been renewed several times. It shows the fight between David and Goliath. A huge Goliath in Roman armour – three storeys tall – is apparently so sure of the battle's outcome that he has propped his elbow coolly on a window, while a tiny David is already swinging his sling.

Back up the street and across Kohlenmarkt (here we cross Route A, p. 24) we reach the centre of power of the former free imperial city, the town hall. This is today composed of the ***New and the Old Town Halls (22)**. We turn first to the New Town Hall, where the heads of the city administration have their offices to the present day. The building was erected on the site of older houses at the end of the 17th century, after the Perpetual Diet had taken over the Old Town Hall, in a then fashionable design with painted corner stones. In a side-room of the Ratskeller restaurant in the same building, you will find plastercasts of the mediaeval figures from the banqueting hall of the Dollinger family (p. 52). Their house, which once stood opposite the Town Hall, was demolished in the 19th century. Right next to the New Town Hall rises the impressive Town Hall Tower, which was, for a long time, the city's highest tower (the cathedral towers were only three storeys high until 1860) and thus clearly proclaimed that this was the city's centre. The layout of the Old Town Hall is exactly the same as that of the houses of the wealthy patricians, i.e. a four-sided building with a tower surrounding a courtyard (c. 1260). On the first floor

Kohlenmarkt with the New and the Old Town Halls in the background

of the tower the remains of yet another formerly open arcade can be seen. Behind it is the room where civil marriages are performed on Thursdays and Fridays in appropriately dignified surroundings. Just like the Italian patricians they wished to emulate, the rich citizens of Regensburg had magnificent ballrooms on the first, i.e. the grandest floor of their houses. Of course the official

A 17th-century painting of the Town Hall complex

representatives of the city did not want to be any less grand. And so around 1360 they erected the huge building with the sumptuously decorated first floor bay-window which stands at right angles to the town hall and houses what was called the **Ball and Debating Room** (the term **Reichssaal**, Imperial Hall, that is used for it today dates back only to the time of the Perpetual Diet). The ground floor was used for offices and business premises, while the cellar was given over to life's darker side, the prison cells and inquisition chamber. The building linking the two complexes, including the portal indicating that this is the town hall, was erected about 50 years later. Two fierce warriors, popularly called 'Schutz' and 'Trutz' (defence and attack), guard the entrance. They also, however, symbolize the privileges of the free imperial city, i.e. the right to protect itself and attack others. The two city crests showing the crossed keys, the symbol of St Peter, indicate for whom they do this. (This motif was printed on the first 80 – pfennig stamp to bear the imprint 'Deutschland' instead of 'Deutsche Post' in 1995, the city's anniversary year.)

The city's old standard measurements are attached to the wall to the left of the portal. In the middle is the city shoe (foot), as can be read above, to the left the ell and, to the right, the 'Klafter', a six-foot measure for wood. Mediaeval measurements were usually based on parts of the body, and so they differed as much from market to market and town to town as they did from person to person. The Regensburg foot was a large one (31.2 cm), the ell, the length of an arm, was shorter than its Bavarian equivalent, whereas the wood measure, the width of spread arms, spans an impressive 1.89 m. These measurements, which were in use until the beginning of the 19th century, were on display in this public location so that people could check they were being used correctly. Napoleon was the first to introduce the metric system all over Europe (with the exception of Great Britain).

The Old Town Hall (p. 82) now houses a museum and can only be visited by taking part in a guided tour (p. 91). Opposite the Imperial Hall, above an old Regensburg public house bearing a famous Munich name, the eye is caught by a statue of a recumbent stag with real antlers. The following legend is attached to it:

The Emperor and the Stag

While the emperor was out hunting one day during an imperial diet, a splendid stag eluded him. It ran into the town and through the open gate of this very house, which at once closed behind it. The angry emperor hammered at the gate and demanded that his quarry be returned to him. But the young daughter of the house pleaded so touchingly for the creature's life that the emperor let her keep it. A statue of it has decorated the facade ever since.

Further to the west, in No 2 Neue Waaggasse, parts of a Romanesque window have been uncovered above the Gothic windows on the first floor. This shows that buildings were repeatedly altered and modernised in the past. Due to this, the true age of most of the city's houses is revealed only in the depth of their cellars.

Haidplatz, where festivities and tournaments used to take place, facing west

Through the gateway of this house we reach the **Fechtschulhof (23)** (courtyard of the fencing school), where fencers practised their art from the 17th century onwards and where Regensburg's pyramid stands today. However, in contrast to the pyramid at the Louvre in Paris, it is not the entrance to a museum but conceals the ventilation shaft of the underground car-park beneath.

At the end of this courtyard, around a further corner and beyond the only children's playground in the historic city centre, we are presented with a view of the reverse of a complex of buildings including no less than three towers. This part of town, the Donauwacht, was the first part of the city to be restored after World War II. The procedure then was very different from what it would be today: without great qualms new window openings were created in the old walls. That would now be out of the question and more recent renovations have been undertaken with far more care.

Nowadays, an analysis of the various layers of plaster covering the facades is also part of the renovation procedure. And as a result of this it has been discovered that most of the facades were colourfully decorated, either with painted window surrounds or borders or even with murals covering the whole facade, as can be seen on the house at No 2 Weingasse, at the end of the square.

To the left, via Weingasse, we reach the city's main square, ****Haidplatz (24)**, which is actually triangular because it lies in a fork in the road. Festivities and tournaments often used to be staged here and the square regained much of its original atmos-

Plaster copy in the New Town Hall of the relief showing the battle between Dollinger and Krako

The Tale of the Battle between Dollinger and Krako

When Emperor Henry I (919 – 936) was staying in Regensburg, a Hungarian delegation came to the city to extend peace treaties. Amongst them was a giant, Krako, who was ten 'shoes' tall. He had a suit of armour made of elephant skin with steel plates nailed to it and his shield was decorated with a mask of the devil. He challenged the knights gathered here to spar with him, and even offered to fight against two knights simultaneously, but no one dared take up such a wager. At this time Hans, the son of the patrician Dollinger family, was in jail for lèse-majesté, which was synonymous with a death-sentence. He alone dared to participate in this unequal duel. Pardoned by the Emperor, he sought out the grave of St Erhard in Niedermünster. There a priest predicted that he would be victorious if he fought under the sign of the cross. The tournament took place in Haidplatz. Hans Dollinger had already been unseated from his horse twice when he remembered the priest's prophecy. Hurriedly, a wooden cross was erected and he promptly won. As the tournament's winner, his opponent's armour as well as his horse was his. He is said to have donated it to Niedermünster Convent, where it was kept until Emperor Charles V requested it and took it to Vienna. Regrettably, it has since been lost. In 1995, during the celebration of the free imperial city's 750th anniversary, the Dollinger legend was performed again on Haidplatz in a modern adaptation.

phere when it ceased to be used as a car park in the 1980s. Behind the Gothic fountain with the statue of Justitia, a massive patrician house from the height of the Gothic period looms up on the square's south-western side; it is known as 'die **Arch**', the ark. It received this name because its shape resembles that of a ship's prow. The red building with the tower at the eastern end of the square became municipal property during the 15th century. The city scales were set up here, and thus the building was named '**Neue Waag**', 'new weighing place'. In the city accounts, there is frequent mention of an expensive institution which was at one time situated in the 'Waag': the city councillors' wine parlour. The building is of historical significance also because ultimately unsuccessful negotiations between Melanchthon and Dr Eck with the aim of reconciling the Protestant and Catholic denominations took place here during the Reformation.

In the Middle Ages there used to be two buildings in the space occupied by the *****Thon-Dittmer-Palais** today. They were bought towards the end of the 18th century by the rich Dittmer family, who were bankers and salt-merchants. The architect Emanuel d'Herigoyen altered the two houses to form an impressive town house with a Classicist facade facing the square, although, behind the facade, much of the old fabric was preserved. In the passage leading through to the courtyard, for instance, a Gothic arch can be spotted on the left. The courtyard's present appearance is partly of a later date. The two old courtyards were already combined into one in Dittmer's time. The Renaissance arcades on the left were preserved. However they were not continued along the north

The courtyard of the Thon-Dittmer-Palais is often used as a backdrop for theatre productions

wing until the 1970s, when the fire brigade moved out of the building and made way for the city's evening school, library and a small theatre, amongst other things. Since then, the courtyard has served as the atmospheric backdrop for open-air performances of music and drama during the summer months (including three weeks of performances by school theatre groups). During the cooler season modern sculptures are put on show here.

Beside the large Gothic arch leading out of the courtyard, on its left as seen from the courtyard, there is a smaller arch leading to the former private chapel dating from around 1380. At the same time a little turret for a clock was constructed above the arch. A little scene such as was popular at the time adorns its base: an old man believes he can rejuvenate himself by having a love-affair with a young girl. But right below is the indication that his efforts are in vain: the Baroque wooden statue of a young woman holding an hour-glass is an allegory of the transience of life. Like the sand in the glass, life trickles by and ends in death, symbolized here by a skull.

Back on Haidplatz, a grey building of castle-like appearance with a seven-storey early Gothic tower stands on the right hand side: the former inn *Zum Goldenen Kreuz (25)* ('The Golden Cross'). From the Middle Ages and up to the end of the last century, it was Regensburg's most luxurious hotel, and many well known people stayed within its walls, amongst them several emperors, for instance, Charles V, Franz Joseph and Wilhelm I.

The Emperor's Last Love Affair

Emperor Charles V (1519 – 56) resided at the Goldenes Kreuz when he came to the city in 1546 for the imperial diet. He was described by his peers as an old, sick man (he was only 46 at the time). Here he met the last great love of his life, the 18-year-old daughter of a girdler, Barbara Blomberg, who proved that he was not so old and sick after all. Nine months after their liaison she gave birth to a healthy son, who was named Don Juan de Austria and was to become a famous man. He defeated the Turkish fleet, which had threatened the whole of the Christian world, in the Battle of Lepanto in the Mediterranean. Barbara Blomberg, later married well and, as the mother of a hero, led an eventful life far from Regensburg.

Ludwigstraße, which leads to Arnulfsplatz, was thus named in 1830 in honour of King Ludwig I of Bavaria. He was staying in Regensburg at that time to participate in the laying of the foundation stone for the Walhalla. In recent years, the Ludwigstraße has regained much of its attractiveness through renovations and superb shops. In the large Gothic patrician house (No 3) a fresco 6 m wide, dating from around 1370 and depicting the Fountain of Youth, was uncovered during restoration on the first floor on the side nearest the road.

Arnulfsplatz (26) was not created until the beginning of the 19th century, when a large square, Jakobshof, was divided into two through the construction of the municipal theatre and the 'Neues Haus', a concert hall.

Regensburg's most popular beer 'oasis', the pub belonging to the Kneitinger brewery, is situated in Arnulfsplatz. Hidden behind it is the **Velodrom (27)**, built in 1897. Its name is taken from its original function. Simon Oberndorfer ran a cycling school here, as learning to cycle involved much effort in those

The Velodrom, now used by Regensburg Theatre

days, just as learning to drive does today. The Velodrom, one of the few big steel constructions of that age to have survived, has a sad history with a happy ending. After being used for decades as a venue for glamorous evening entertainment, it was converted into a cinema. Once the cinema had closed down in the 70s, the building gradually deteriorated and was even going to be demolished. Through the initiative of private citizens, however, it was saved at the last minute. Since its successful renovation by a private benefactor, it has provided a further venue for Regensburg Theatre's productions, although it is also used for other events.

Route C
From West to East – right through the Centre
From the Scottish monks to the Dominicans, via Gesandtenstraße to the Neupfarrplatz, the former ghetto, from the cathedral precinct to that of the dukes and from the Minorites to the eastern city gate and the Königliche Villa. (Town plan inside front cover)

Only the two flanking towers at the end of Schottenstraße have survived as a reminder of the old city gate (c. 1300), the western boundary of the mediaeval city. The rest had to make way for the traffic, which also caused part of the damage to the world-famous ***Schottenportal (28) (Scots' Portal). Its mysterious composition of figures has puzzled generations of scholars. Many highly complicated and involved interpretations of this Romanesque cycle of sculptures had been suggested.

Although the sculptures are undoubtedly Romanesque, they were probably placed here in this arrangement at a later date. A glass porch has been erected in front of the portal and its carvings

in order to prevent further deterioration until they can be restored.

The massive **Schottenkirche St. Jakob (28) (Scottish Church of St James) was the mother church of all the monasteries of Scottish monks in Bavaria and Austria.

Detail of the figures surrounding the west doorway of the Schottenkirche

Interior of the Schottenkirche

In its present form it dates mainly from 1150 to 1200. The impressive interior with its imaginative capitals was fitted with a coffered ceiling in the 17th century. 19th-century restoration work removed Baroque elements, the frescoes in the east choir and the glass windows were restored. Today, furnishings from various churches adorn the interior. The crucifixion group in the triumphal arch dates back to the time the church was constructed, the Virgin on the choir pillar to around 1360. Before we leave the church again, we see the prostrate figure of the porter Rydan to the right of the portal. It was his duty to lock the church up securely with a bar and key, as the monastery lay outside the city walls when it was first built. From 1577 to 1599 Ninian Winzet, who was father confessor to Mary Stuart, was abbot of the monastery, which was not dissolved until 1866, and he is also buried here.

Rydan – the stone porter in St Jakob's Church

Bismarckplatz with the Theater

Bismarckplatz (29), like Arnulfsplatz (p. 55), was not created until the beginning of the 19th century. It is dominated by two Classicist buildings with magnificent porticos, the municipal theatre and the former Präsidialpalais (presidential palace), which today houses the police headquarters. The **Präsidialpalais** on the square's southern side was built in 1804/05 for the French ambassador to the Perpetual Diet at the behest of Prince-primate Carl von Dalberg (1803 – 1810) by his court architect, Emmanuel d'Herigoyen.

The **Theatre**, which was created simultaneously as 'a new public theatre and assembly room' was destroyed by a fire barely 50 years after its construction. Shortly afterwards it was rebuilt in the same style as before. The theatre has recently been refurbished and, equipped with the very latest technology, has now been restored to its original splendour.

To the left of the Präsidialpalais, set back a little from the square, stands the ***Dominican church of St Blasius (30)**. The Dominicans came to Regensburg in 1229, just after the Franciscans (p. 72). Since both were mendicant orders and thus dependent on donations from locals, they built their churches far apart, as was also the case in many other towns, one in the west, one in the east of the city. This was the only way of ensuring that they did not hinder each other while collecting donations. According to the order's rules, the Dominican church had to be built simply and austerely, expensive decoration and even a steeple were prohibited. After the dissolution of the adjoining monastery at the beginning of the 19th century, the church became the church of the Marian Men's Congregation; it can only be visited before services and during guided tours which take place at the weekend during the summer months.

The small square in front of it was named after **Albertus Magnus**, the famous Dominican monk who lectured here from 1237 to 1240. During a brief interlude, from 1260 to 1962, he was bishop of Regensburg; after that, however, he withdrew to concentrate exclusively on his theological studies.

When the construction of an underground car park under Bismarckplatz was planned at the end of the 1970s, the archaeologists seized the opportunity to excavate. And as has so often been the case in Regensburg, fascinating things came to light. Some foundations and painted walls of houses with smoking chambers and limekilns proved that the Roman village (cannabae) which usually existed near a legionary fort had stood here. The archaeologists made a further sensational discovery (which is today in the Historical Museum, p. 81): the skeletons of four horses with their heads cut off, together with decorative gilt horse brasses from the creatures' harnesses, dating from around A.D. 600. Probably they were part of the burial treasures of an important Agilolfing nobleman and were buried with him true to the customs of the time. After the underground car park had been completed, Bismarckplatz was newly paved and fountains were installed. On Saturdays a market selling country produce is held here, and in summer the square is a popular meeting place, alive with people of all generations until far into the night.

The interior of the Dominican church of St Blasius

The **Gesandtenstraße** (Ambassadors' Street) follows the course of a Roman street, the one leading from the fort's western gate to the Via Augustana, which came from the south, from Augsburg. It was given its present name at the end of the 18th century, probably because so many ambassadors to the Perpetual Diet lived along it or in the vicinity.

The very first house on the right, on the corner of Bismarck-platz, for instance, was the embassy of the Duchy of Württem-berg. Further on along the street on the right there is a large three-sided complex (No 13), which once housed the imperial free city's grammar school. Whereas during the Middle Ages practically only monastery schools had existed, an increasing number of municipal schools were established from the 16th century onwards.

The **Gymnasium Poeticum (31)** was founded in 1505 and moved to this building, which the city had purchased a few years beforehand, in 1537. It remained here until 1875. The western part, which is today occupied by the State Library, was rebuilt from 1728 onwards, the eastern section was refurbished in 1901/02 by German Bestelmeyer. It is called the Alumneum because pupils (Lat. alumni) from outside Regensburg could lodge here.

The *Dreieinigkeitskirche (32) (Church of the Holy Trinity) was the first purpose-built Protestant church of the early Baroque period (1627 – 31) and has the typical galleries in its interior. The

visitor should, if possible, go up the tower. From up there one has a wonderful view of the intricate roofscape and can spot some of the roof-gardens which, invisible from below, make life in the city centre so desirable. The small cemetery adjoining the church is also worth a visit. The inscriptions on the splendid 17th and 18th century

The interior of the Protestant Dreieinigkeitskirche

tombstones indicate that, above all, ambassadors to the Perpetual Diet were buried here. Sadly, the large mediaeval complex (Nos 3/5), called the ***Zant- and Ingolstetterhaus (33)** unfortunately used to be in a very poor state of repair, but the refurbishment of the enormous building has at last been completed. The complex is a unique monument not only because of architectural elements ranging from Romanesque features to Rococo alterations, but also because of the various uses it has been put to.

When the Bernard brothers bought it in 1812, two patrician houses, including towers and outbuildings in the area of the Zanthaus, had already been combined to provide space for the chancellery, the archives and the library of the Thurn und Taxis family. The Bernards turned the building into a snuff factory without undertaking significant structural alterations and extended it to include the Ingolstetterhaus in the 19th

Old machinery for the production of snuff at the Zant- and Ingolstetterhaus

century. The snuff they produced attained worldwide fame and, until a few years ago, was manufactured in the building. The firm not only left its premises unaltered but was also conservative in its treatment of its already historic machinery. Now that the huge complex of buildings has been renovated, this machinery has been placed in a small museum and offers visitors a chance to learn about 19th-century working life as well as the production of snuff.

The western gate of the Roman military fort stood in the area between Bachgasse (here we cross Route A, p. 24) and Wahlenstraße.

Beyond it is **Neupfarrplatz (34)**, with the Neupfarrkirche in the middle. Until 1519 this was the location of the Jewish ghetto (p. 13). Alterations to the square were begun in 1994. The square was going to be turned from a car park into a pedestrian area of market-like character. The time allocated for these operations was brief. However, once more the planners had failed to foresee all eventualities. The archaeologists had been given plenty of time for excavations and had turned up nothing spectacular before the

Sparkasse built its new banking centre (No 6a) in 1993, and so the planners were fairly sure that nothing of interest would be found underneath Neupfarrplatz. A circular bunker had been built here in 1939, during World War II, thoroughly destroying, it was presumed, all remains of earlier times. After most of the square had already been repaved, the archaeologists discovered Romanesque cellar walls superimposed on Roman walls (s. document Neupfarrplatz, p. 78) during preliminary excavations in connection with the laying of public utility systems. The discovery turned into a sensation when the fountain to the west of the church was dismantled for restoration. The foundations of the synagogue were revealed underneath it. The masonry was carefully documented but then covered over again in order to protect it from weathering. Dani Karavan designed a modern monument made of white concrete for the site of the synagogue. His intention was to create a meeting-place for all the different cultures and religions and this has indeed proved very popular with the public.

The development around the square is not uniform. Here, many of the older houses were stripped of their facades or even demolished and replaced by new buildings during the wave of modernisation after World War II. Sometimes part of an old facade was integrated – as a fig leaf so to speak –, as was the case with the house once occupied by the City Watch on the east side of the square. The ***Löschenkohl-Palais** (No 14), alone, regained its former splendour after being renovated in 1988. Being Protestants, the Löschenkohl family came to the Protestant free imperial city from Catholic Austria around 1600. Despite the city´s desolate financial state, the family succeeded in acquiring wealth and reputation through bank dealings and commerce. In about 1730 the plan was set in motion to have a splendid town house erected in the best Viennese tra-

The view of the Cathedral from Neupfarrplatz

dition by the Austrian architect Michael Prunner. But shortly after its completion Löschenkohl went bankrupt and the mansion was let to the ambassador of the Electoral Principality of Saxony at the Perpetual Diet. Today it is, as it originally was, a bank.

From the north-eastern corner of the square one reaches the cathedral square via Residenzstraße, where two impressive patrician houses stand on the left opposite the cathedral facade. At the time of their construction (around 1300) they formed a single complex, built by the wealthy and powerful 'Hansgraf', a kind of minister of commerce for the rich trading city. The left-hand part is today called **Haus Heuport (35)**, since hay was once sold here in front of the small gate leading to the Jewish ghetto.

The other part, the **Kaiserhof**, was not named after the supreme sovereign of the empire: Kaiser was simply the family name of the house's owner. At first-floor level Haus Heuport has a row of decorative windows in purest Venetian Gothic style. Behind them lay the owners' private ballroom. Baroque wooden stairs lead up to it from the courtyard. At the bottom of the stairs, on the right, is a stone with three round indentations. Torches had to be extinguished there before mounting the stairs, to reduce the risk of fire. On the left-hand corner of the wall, there are two little statues dating from around 1330 which tell another of the little stories that were so popular in the Middle Ages (on the same topic see 'Sermon to the Geese' p. 45 and Thon-Dittmer-Hof p. 53).

Seducer and Seduced

The statues are of a young man and girl. He is marked out as a suitor by the apple in his hand. The girl he is courting is obviously enchanted, as her smile shows. But the young man has no serious intentions, as can be seen from behind. There, we see a snake slithering out of his open gown. Perhaps the scene was meant to be a warning to the citizens' daughters to be circumspect and not to let themselves be tempted when they came here on festive occasions. It is a unique group in that the apple and the snake are attributed to a man and not, as is usual, to Eve.

The **Residenz** (Residence, No 6 Domplatz) only served as such for seven years although it kept its name. From 1803 to 1810, Prince-primate Carl von Dalberg resided at the Cathedral Provost's House, which had been newly built only three years before in the Classicist style. The most important guest to stay at the house was Na-poleon, who set up his headquarters here for two days in 1809 and received the local dignitaries. The Gothic *****Cathedral of St Peter (36)**, the city's episcopal church, has had a somewhat speck-led appearance since it was recently cleaned. This is because of the different sorts of stone used in its construction: first, a type of limestone, then green sandstone for the 19th-century additions and, for the pieces replaced in the last three decades, limestone again, which can still be identified by its lighter colour. All these types of stone are 'soft' and thus easy to work with, but also more susceptible to pollution. The damage to the cathedral – as documented by early photographs – increased from c. 1900. This was not the fault of industry or the traffic – both were not yet present to a notable degree in Regensburg – but a result of the burning of domestic fuel. Even the largest houses had previously had only one or two fireplaces, now every room was fitted with a stove.

Even today no method has been found to preserve the stones effectively and for long periods. It is, however, not only the building material which gives the cathedral's facade an uneven look. The windows at the bottom of the towers also vary greatly. During the main period of construction, which lasted for about 250 years (from c. 1274 to c. 1520), many architects worked on the cathedral. Each one of them built his part in the style of the day. Until the middle of the 19th century, the towers only had three storeys and square sloping roofs. King Ludwig I, builder of the Walhalla and the

The facade of the Cathedral of St Peter with its twin spires

Befreiungshalle, had both towers raised by one storey and the spires added. Since then, at a height of 105 m, they have been the highest towers in the historic city centre.

The cathedral facade tells many tales in a variety of ways. Statues, gargoyles, reliefs and stained-glass windows tell those who are able to decipher them not only about the history of the world and of religion, but also about the mediaeval picture of the world. A few examples will demonstrate this: on the facade, in a central position directly below the crucifix, a carving shows the patron saint of the cathedral, Saint Peter, sitting in a boat and holding the keys which are his attribute (arranged to form a cross, of course, they eventually became Regensburg's city crest). In the tympanum of the small right-hand portal he appears again. Here the sculptor shows Peter's release from prison in a naive manner by simply having an angel lift the roof off the building. A very different theme is indicated by the four figures on horseback in front of the pillars. The heathen rulers of four great empires are shown – Nebuchadnezzar on a bear, Alexander the Great on a panther, Augustus on a unicorn and Cyrus on a lion. But why? In this way the cathedral expresses its claim to be the heir to all these empires. On the third pillar of the southern nave, by contrast, is a controversial relief, the 'Jewish sow'. The mediaeval church fought Judaism vigorously, using many means, in this case, insulting mockery. The question whether this relief is a historical document which ought to be preserved as such or a piece of anti–Semitic abuse which should be removed has led time and again to heated discussions.

The interior of the cathedral

We enter the cathedral today by the south door.
Opening times: April to Oct: 9 – 6; Nov to March: 10 – 4; on Sundays and holidays, access for visitors only from 12 noon onwards (p. 91).

Once our eyes have become accustomed to the dark interior, the colourful glass windows begin to glow. Here, the whole development of stained glass can be traced. The mediaeval window panes are assembled like precious mosaics from small pieces of coloured glass linked together by black leading. Windows decorate the choir, the transept and the aisles. The oldest window panes in the south transept in fact date back to the Romanesque cathedral (c. 1230). Work on the window glass continued until about 1470. Then there was a 400-year break until King Ludwig I donated the windows in the west front. These 19th-century windows look completely different. They are no longer made up of small pieces, but of large glass panels painted with glass paint. When the newest window in the north aisle, the Whitsun window, was inserted (in 1988), the original technique was again applied.

The interior of the cathedral, as it presents itself today, is the result of the 'purification' process in the 19th century and renovation work in the 1980s. To make the cathedral 'purely Gothic' again, almost everything that was not Gothic was removed from the cathedral about 150 years ago (p. 71). Only few works of art, like the huge tomb of Cardinal Philipp Wilhelm of Bavaria in the middle of the nave (made in 1611 by Hans Krumper) or the high altar, survived this wave of purification. It took almost a century (1695 – 1785) for the altar to acquire its present form through individual donations from bishops and canons. It is the work of Augsburg goldsmiths. The bishops' crypt, which can be reached by a flight of steps opposite the entrance, dates from the 1980s.

As is the case during most building operations in Regensburg, new discoveries were made during its construction. A row of round Romanesque pillars was uncovered, part of an arcaded walk bordering the courtyard between the old cathedral (pp. 13, 44) and the baptistry, which stood roughly where the cathedral's facade stands today. Apart from its outstanding stained-glass windows, the cathedral also has well-known stone sculptures. The most famous is certainly the Smiling Angel, which is part of the Annunciation Group by the Erminold Master (c. 1280). Nowadays the group is at-

The later of two stained-glass windows depicting the saints appealed to in times of distress

tached to the two pillars on the right and left of the crossing in the nave. Originally, both figures were colourfully painted and the angel carried the Christ Child on its arm. Altogether, the interior of the cathedral presented a more colourful appearance than to-day, as was proved by examinations during the most recent resto-ration. Apart from the statues, certain structural elements were painted, for instance the cross-ribs of the vaulting. Further well-known pieces of stonework which deserve to be mentioned are the tabernacle and the well (both by Wolfgang Roritzer, late 15th cen-tury) and the two small figures in the niches on either side of the main portal in the west wall. They are popularly known as 'the devil and his grandmother', but are really demonic creatures who were supposed to deter evil forces from entering the church.

Regensburg Cathedral has another very different claim to fame: its choir, the world-famous Regensburger Domspatzen, the 'Cathedral Sparrows', who have been serving the cathedral for more than a thousand years. From the third year of primary school until they leave school, they receive a musical education at their own, state-approved school. Though they are famous mainly for their world-wide concert-tours, they are primarily a cathedral choir. And to the present day they sing the Lord's praises every Sunday during high mass (10 a.m.). Amongst the many special services, the Christmas Mass on Christmas Eve deserves particular mention as one of the cathedral's most impressive events.

The post office opposite the cathedral was built in the 19th centu-ry in place of several cathedral canons' houses, but the original splendid decorations on its facade were removed in the 20th cen-tury. A flower market takes place on weekdays around the modern fountain (by Fritz König) dedicated to Albrecht Altdorfer, Regensburg's most fa-mous painter, which is situated a little way to the east.

The Smiling Angel from the Annunciation Group by the Erminold Master

Right beside the cathedral choir is the next church, that of ***St Ulrich (37)**, built around 1225/30. It stands between the cathedral precinct and that of the dukes which started immediately behind it. It was originally built as the dukes' palace chapel, but was first used as the cathedral parish church just a decade later, and continued to be used as such until the church was deconsecrated in 1824. The bulls'-eye windows were inserted into the walls of this early Gothic building during the Baroque period; today it serves as the diocesan museum (p. 82) and is at the same time parish church of the cathedral chapter.

Between the cathedral and St Ulrich's, a wide gateway leads to the cathedral garden. On the right-hand side is the stonemasons' workshop, where up to the present day damaged pieces of masonry from the cathedral are repaired by the cathedral's master builder and about a dozen masons using traditional techniques. The cathedral cloisters adjoined the Romanesque cathedral to the north (p. 13). When the Gothic cathedral was rebuilt in a slightly more westerly position, the connection was made by a flying buttress. Between the cathedral cloisters and the stonemasons' work-shop, a path leads east to the ***Niedermünster (38)**, once a religious foundation for noblewomen, which became the residence of Regensburg's bishops after the foundation's dissolution at the beginning of the 19th century. Although the complex looks like a convent, the ladies who lived here were not nuns. Daughters of noble families who could not be, or were not intended to be, married off, as well as widows, lived here together from the 9th century on under fairly liberal circumstances, as is proved by the existence of a number of love-letters, which were admittedly felt to be scandalous. The former convent church – which is today the cathedral parish church – has a long history. Despite many fires and alterations, numerous objets d'art from various centuries have survived. The church's Romanesque towers dominate the city even from a distance.

The vestibule with the tombstones of the convent's abbess-

The interior of St Ulrich's Church

es, which was altered in Baroque times, hides a Romanesque portal with impressive door-knockers, large, beautifully executed Romanesque lion-masks. The interior of the church, which was also altered according to Baroque taste, revealed a glimpse of the city's most distant past when a plan for a new heating system during the 1960s led to excavations underneath the building. The discoveries made spanned many centuries, ranging from the foundations of Roman military barracks, constructed first from wood, then, later, from stone, to a Roman sarcophagus containing the remains of St Erhard, and to the remains of an ecclesiastical building dating from Agilolfing and then Romanesque times. *(Restoration work is currently in progress here, but it will be possible to view the excavations again in 2009.)*

From the church portal to the left via Niedermünstergasse, we reach **Alter Kornmarkt (39)** (Old Cornmarket), where a corn market was held up to about 1830. This was originally the duke's domain. The duke's palace, the Römerturm or Heidenturm (Roman or Heathen Tower) and his palace chapel, the so-called *****Alte Kapelle** (Old Chapel) are proof of this. The latter building can hardly be called a chapel, as it takes up the whole of the southern side of the square. Emperor Henry II, who was later canonized, had a large Romanesque basilica erected here just after the turn of the millennium, and its nave still stands today. Roman stone blocks were also re-used for its construction. The elevated choir was added in Gothic times. The building's somewhat strange outward appearance is due to the 'double bass windows', which were inserted when the interior of the church was redecorated in Rococo times. Following recent renovation, the church's interior is once more resplendent in the style of Bavarian Rococo. The nave and choir had been completely redecorated by local and regional artists in less than thirty years during the 18th century. The main part of the church is reached through a vestibule which bears witness to its history and contains the Romanesque font in a chapel to the left; the church's decoration becomes more splendid as one draws near the choir and reaches its climax in the high altar. The frescoes in the nave and transept show the story of two saints, Emperor Henry II and his wife Kunigunde. The ceiling fresco shows Pope Benedict VIII presenting an icon of the Virgin Mary to the Emperor on the occasion of his coronation in Rome. Henry gave the painting, which according to legend was the work of St Luke the Evangelist, to the Alte Kapelle, which is why the church bears the name 'Our Lady'. Up to the present day the picture (a 13th century copy according to recent research), which is held to have miraculous powers, is worshipped in the south side chapel. The ceiling fresco in the south transept shows a scene from the life of Empress Kunigunde. Accused of adultery, she proved her innocence by walking barefoot over ploughshares. When a donor offered to present Pope Benedict XVI with an organ, he decided to have it installed in the city where he had lived and worked for many years and, more specifically, in the Alte Kapelle. During his pontifical visit to Bavaria, he personally consecrated this organ on September 13, 2006, naming it the Pope Benedict Organ.

On the western side of the Alter Kornmarkt stands the **Herzogshof** (Duke's Palace). The present building dates from the 13th century, with later alterations. A flying buttress links it with the **Römerturm** (Roman Tower), also known as the **Heidenturm** (Heathen Tower). The base of this 28 m high tower, which was built in Carolingian times, has walls 4 m thick. It probably served as a treasure chamber and also as a stronghold in case of danger. Until the 19th century it was accessible only from the Herzogshof via the flying buttress. The adjoining building was already being used as a smithy in the 14th century. Horses were shod in the wooden shelter in front of it.

Though the Wittelsbach dukes gave up their residence after Regensburg had become a free imperial city in 1245, the Herzogshof and the square in front of it remained Bavarian property; in consequence Bavarian law was, curiously enough, applicable here in

Alter Kornmarkt with the Duke's Palace and the Alte Kapelle

The choir of the Alte Kapelle

the city centre, until 1902, when the square became the property of the city.

On the eastern side of the square stands the **Karmelitenkirche** (Carmelite Church), the only purely Baroque church building in the centre. Emperor Ferdinand II had called the 'Barefoot' Carmelites to the city in 1634 in the course of the Counter Reformation. However, the city council made it a condition that a local architect must be employed to build the new church. Since the Carmelites wanted a church after the Italian fashion, however, they named their abbot as the architect and officially employed the unknown Italian architect as an interpreter, because supposedly the abbot spoke no German. When the church and monastery were dissolved in 1810, the buildings served for a time as a toll house and prison. But the Carmelites returned as early as 1836. The church was now furnished with altars from various churches; the main and side altars were brought here from the Cathedral.

Local people are convinced that the Carmelite liqueur produced here in the monastery is a medicine that cures all illnesses. The herb liqueur, which is still made by the monks according to a recipe which is kept strictly secret and passed on only orally, is sold right beside the church. To the left of the church, Pfluggasse leads to Schwanenplatz, which was created after World War II, when a whole group of houses was demolished. The massive stone

The former Minorite church now houses the Historical Museum

blocks visible in the walls of the houses on the left are remnants of the eastern wall of the Roman fort.

Diagonally across the square, at its southern end, is the former ***Minoritenkirche (40)** (Minorite Church) and the monastery connected to it. At the time of its construction in the 13th century (the east choir was built in the mid-14th century), it still stood outside the city walls. Being the church of a mendicant order, it is as austere as the Dominicans' church (p. 58). The church and the former monastery house the city's vast collections (Historical Museum p. 81). In Bertholdstraße, named after the famous preacher who attracted so many listeners that he had to preach his sermons outdoors, is the ***Leerer Beutel (41)** (Empty Bag), a former grain store. The city was obliged to provide its citizens with a supply of corn large enough to ensure that no one had to go hungry during the turmoils of war and the recurring wheat embargoes with which the Bavarian dukes used to put pressure on the free imperial city. Where the nickname for the grain store came from is not completely clear, but it probably derives from the invitation to would-be buyers to empty their purses. Since its restoration in 1980 it has become a cultural centre with permanent and short-term art exhibitions, a film theatre, live jazz and a popular restaurant.

The Dancing Bear and the Beer of the Brandlbräu

An itinerant circus with a dancing bear is said to have stayed at the house on one occasion. When a thief attempted to steal two calves one night, he met the bear, which barred his way until the publican had been woken by the noise. Out of gratitude he bought the dancing bear from the troupe, kept it as a pet and duly increased his beer sales thanks to the custom attracted by his exotic possession.

Ostengasse (42) is the continuation of the road running parallel to the Danube (Route B, p. 42) in the direction of Straubing, Passau and Vienna. The buildings along it were suburban in character. Here instead of tall, massive patrician mansions, there are the small, low houses of artisans and traders. In addition to these this street had about a dozen inns and brewery pubs until the 19th century, obviously to cater for the travellers arriving in the city. At the **Brandlbräu** (No 16), the house with the chained bear, brewing ceased just thirty-five years ago. The *****Ostentor (43)** (East Gate, c. 1300) is the only city gate belonging to the mediaeval fortifications which has been completely preserved.

The Ostentor, the fortified east gate of the mediaeval city

The Königliche Villa (Royal Villa)

While the facade facing the town has a relatively large number of windows, its outer wall is dauntingly blank. Beyond the gate and the watchman's house, the Villa Park, which was created on top of the former fortifications and trenches, opens out towards the Danube. Since King Maximilian II of Bavaria wished to have a befitting residence in Regensburg, Ludwig Foltz was commissioned to build the **Königliche Villa (42)** (Royal Villa) in 1854. It took two years to construct the neo-Gothic building, which accommodated royal guests only about half a dozen times before the end of the monarchy. Through the park we reach the Danube and can return to the city centre via the path along the river bank and across Donaumarkt (Route B, p. 42).

...other Places of Interest

Regensburg's surroundings also offer many attractions, three of which will be described here:

An Outing to the ** Walhalla (45)

Opening hours: 9 – 5.45 from April to Sept; 9 – 4.45 in Oct; 10 – 11.45 and 1.00 – 3.45 from Nov to March. www.walhalla-regensburg.de

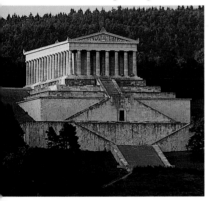

The Walhalla at Donaustauf

The Walhalla (1830 – 1842) in Donaustauf can be reached by boat (from the Steinerne Brücke), by bus or car. As crown prince, King Ludwig I had already developed plans to build a suitably grand monument in honour of famous members of the German–speaking world. After long deliberation he chose a hillside overlooking the Danube, a river of great historical significance, as the location for his project, one within sight of Regensburg, the city of emperors and kings. It was decided that the monument should take the form of a Greek temple, which Leo von Klenze, Ludwig's architect, then built between 1830 and 1841, taking the Parthenon in Athens as his model. The best way of visiting the Walhalla is by climbing the huge stairway (358 steps) leading up to it (it is however also possible to drive to a signposted car park behind the building; from there the monument can be reached via a path with far fewer steps). After the Napoleonic Wars and the end of the Holy Roman Empire, the king's aim was to give the German nation, which was now divided up into many small states, a hall of fame to restore its self-confidence. The interior, a hall splendidly adorned with multi-coloured marble, contains 128 busts as well as 65 inscribed tablets. The tablets were dedicated to people whose appearance and even whose name was no longer known, for instance the master builder of Cologne Cathedral or the three Swiss men who swore the Oath of Rütli. Ludwig himself selected 150 candidates for inclusion before the Walhalla was inaugurated. Even nowadays, solemn ceremonies are held every few years and personalities deemed worthy of the honour are inducted into the hall of fame. Besides his or her fame, the other conditions for inclusion are that a person has been dead for five years and was a German-speaker. The selection is made by the Bavarian Council of Ministers.

Kelheim and the **Befreiungshalle (Hall of Liberation) (46)**

Visitors can walk up to the Befreiungshalle either from the car park beside the landing-stage for boats to Weltenburg (a fairly steep climb) or from the car park to the west of the hall, which is open from 9 a.m. to 4 p.m in winter and from 9 a.m. to 6 p.m. in summer.
www.schloesser.bayern.de

An ancient area of human settlement is to be found near Kelheim, about 28 km west of Regensburg and also on the Danube. The Altmühl and the Danube flow together here and there was a major Celtic settlement, an oppidum, on the Michaelsberg between the two rivers. When, shortly after the ceremonial opening of the Walhalla, King Ludwig I of Bavaria wished to erect a memorial for the German troops in the Wars of Liberation from Napoleon and for all Germans, he chose this particular site because of its historic associations. The Battle of the Nations at Leipzig on October 18, 1813, in which cooperation between the German states made the decisive victory against Napoleon possible, is frequently referred to in the design of the building. Visible from far away, the monument, which stands on a high plinth and has 18 sides at its base, has 18 pillars around its walls. Female figures on these pillars symbolise the 18 German tribes which participated in the Wars of Liberation. Above, there is a colonnade consisting of 3 groups of 18 columns and then,

slightly further back, another 18 pillars, here crowned by trophies. Although it was built of brick, the hall was rendered and painted in such a way that it looks as if large blocks of marble were used. When one has climbed the flight of 84 steps leading to the entrance, there is an enormous doorway leading into a domed hall that is 49 m high. Here, everything that looks like marble really is marble. A splendid example of the crafts-

The Hall of Liberation near Kelheim

man's work is the floor inlaid with the admonition: 'May the Germans never forget what necessitated the struggle for liberation and how they won it!'
18 niches on a plinth running all round the hall divide up the lower part of it. In front are 34 goddesses of victory who either grasp each other's hands or carry a bronze shield on which the victorious battles in the Wars of Liberation are named. Each of the larger-than-lifesize statues is different. Tablets above the top of each niche are engraved with the

names of military commanders, while others directly above the colonnade give the names of conquered fortresses. The cupola opens into a glass lantern almost 6 m high and 8 m wide. This is the only source of light in the hall – apart from the opened doors. From the outside plinth, a flight of stairs leads to the colonnade around the interior and also to the external balustrade. From both of them, there is a magnificent view. The foundation stone was laid in 1842 and building work began in 1843, initially under the supervision of Friedrich von Gärtner and then of Leo von Klenze. After Ludwig abdicated in 1848, as a result of the March Revolution and of his liaison with Lola Montez, building stopped for a while, but was then continued, now at Ludwig's own expense. The hall also remained his private property until his death. The ceremonial opening took place on the 50th anniversary of the Battle of Leipzig and was attended by all the surviving commanders from the Wars of Liberation.

Kelheim, a small Bavarian town once ruled by dukes, is rather like a Roman camp in that its two main streets intersect in the town centre. The former ducal residence lies in the south-eastern part of the town, between the Altmühl and the Danube. It is particularly worth going to see the old established wheat-beer brewery, the museum with its Celtic treasures and the Ludwig Canal, which flows west of the old town. Twelve hundred years

ago, Charlemagne dreamed of linking the Danube and the Main, and thus also the Rhine, by means of a man-made waterway, but we do not know if this project was completed at that time. King Ludwig I of Bavaria did manage to do it. The canal he built, however, was not a great success since the railway arrived at just the same time and was, quite simply, faster and more convenient. Moreover, his canal was very narrow, even for those times; if one compares it with the modern Main-Danube Canal, which flows to the east and north of the town centre, it looks like a miniature waterway.

**Weltenburg Abbey and the Danube Gorge (47)

Weltenburg Abbey can be reached either by ship (in 40 minutes from Kelheim to Weltenburg, in 20 minutes from Weltenburg to Kelheim; during the season, departures every 45 minutes on weekdays, every 30 minutes at the weekends, www.renate.de) or on foot from the car park in Weltenburg (approx. 1 km). The abbey church is open during the daytime except when the Benedictine monks are holding services.
www.weltenburg.de

Weltenburg Abbey is one of the most ancient monastic foundations in Bavaria and dates from the early 7th century. Columban monks were the first to arrive, followed by the Benedictines. The exposed position near the Danube Gorge led, apart from damage caused by military action, to repeated problems as a result of almost regular floods. At the beginning of the 18th century, both the monastery buildings and the church needed to be completely rebuilt. The church itself, begun in 1716 and one of the smallest abbey churches in Bavaria, is the first one that the Asam Brothers were able to plan and build from scratch, with Cosmos Damian acting as the architect and painter and Egid Quirin as the stucco-plasterer. And here, too, they show what they had learned in Rome. From outside, the church betrays nothing of its fabulous baroque interior. A light grey, relatively flat facade leads one to expect a simple church with a nave and two aisles. Inside, though, it is not at all like that. A 'teatrum sacrum' captivates both worshippers and visitors. When one enters the low porch, one immediately catches sight of a figure on horseback riding out from the bright, indirectly illuminated chancel. This is St George, the church's patron saint, who is killing the dragon and thus saving the maiden. The scene is flanked on either side by twisted pillars like those created by Bernini for the tabernacle in St Peter's in Rome. From the porch, the oval-shaped main section of the church seems fairly dark; only on entering, is the brilliant three-tiered design revealed. The lowest zone is linked with the ground and is appropriately earth-coloured; then, a concave ceiling (like the lowest part of a cupola), already much more strongly coloured in white, gold and green, leads one's gaze up to a really bright, though again indirectly lit, painted ceiling. Apart from showing the coronation of the Virgin Mary, saints, apostles and figures from the Old Testament, this also features the Abbot of Weltenburg and some of

View of Weltenburg Abbey with the Danube Gorge in the foreground

his monks. Here, too, as in nearly all Asam churches, the two brothers portrayed themselves for posterity: Egid Quirin is to be seen on the painted ceiling as the personification of genius, Cosmas Damian appears lower down as an observer in courtly dress between the balustrade and the coronet-like ring around the base of the ceiling in the chancel. The monastery buildings still house the abbey brewery, where – according to tradition – a delicious dark beer has been brewed ever since 1050. This may be sampled on the spot in the abbey's own restaurant or in the popular beergarden.

The Danube Gorge

The 'Weltenburger Enge', the stretch of the Danube from just below the abbey down to Kelheim, is officially protected as an area of natural beauty and it was awarded a European Diploma in 1976. This section of the river, 5.5 km long and 400 m wide, is flanked by cliffs up to 40 m high with lots of small caves in them. The limestone rock formations have acquired such evocative names as the Three Quarrelling Brothers, the Roman Cliffs, the Stone Maiden, and Peter and Paul. The best way to experience this jewel is to travel by boat to Kelheim, a 20-minute trip. In the actual gorge, between the so-called 'Calm Rock-Face' and the 'Long Rock-Face', the width of the river is reduced in the range of 110m.

A particularly pleasant trip, which can last half a day or up to a whole day, depending on the time spent in (for example) the restaurant or beergarden at Weltenburg, begins at the car park next to the landing-stage in Kelheim. From here, the path goes over the Ludwig Canal and up to the Befreiungshalle. From the car park there, an archaeological trail (5 km long) leads to the bank of the Danube opposite Weltenburg, where small boats wait to ferry visitors across to the abbey. After visiting the abbey and sampling the delicacies in the restaurant, you can take the ship back to Kelheim.

Museums

Regensburg's varied selection of museums and art galleries are well worth visiting – and not only in bad weather! They are listed here in alphabetical order. Note: the post code for the city centre to the south of the Danube is 93047; only differing postcodes are included in the addresses below; Regensburg's telephone dialling code is 0049 941 (from abroad) or 0941 (from within Germany).

Brückturmmuseum (Bridge Tower Museum) (48)

At the southern end of the Steinerne Brücke, Weisse-Lamm-Gasse 1 tel. 5 07 58 89; www.regensburg.de Open: daily 10 – 5 from April to Oct. Displays and information about the history of the Stone Bridge as well as shipping on the Danube. Also offers splendid views of Regensburg's roofscape.

document Neupfarrplatz (49)

Entrance on north side of Neupfarrkirche. Special tours by arrangement, tel. 5 07 34 42 or museumsfuehrungen@regensburg.de

Open: Thur, Fri, Sat at 2.30, July and August also Sun and Mon at 2.30 (guided tours only). Tickets on sale at Tabak Götz, Neupfarrplatz 3.
The cellars of the former Jewish ghetto house an exhibition of objects dating from the past 2000 years, i.e. from Roman times to the Nazi era, that were all found

Cellars in document Neupfarrplatz

at this site. There is also a multimedia show illustrating the varied history of this part of Regensburg.

document Schnupftabakfabrik (Snuff Factory) (48)

Gesandtenstraße 3, www.regensburg.de Guided tours only: Friday at 2.30; Sat and Sun at 11 and 2.30; tickets available from 'Tee- und Schokoladenhaus Hornung' next door. Advance booking for private tours: tel. 5 07 34 42 or museumsfuehrungen@regensburg.de
The museum on the ground-floor of these historic buildings provides all sorts of information about the production of snuff and has rare, original machinery on display.

The two ships belonging to the Shipping Museum

Domschatzmuseum (Cathedral Treasury Museum) (51)

*Krautermarkt 3
tel. 5 76 45, fax 5 95 32 25 31
www.bistumsmuseen-regensburg.de
Access via the courtyard of the Bischofshof or the cathedral's north transept. Open: April to Oct – Tues to Sat from 10 – 5, Sun and hols from 12 – 5; Dec to March – Fri and Sat 10 – 4, Sun and hols from 12 – 4.*
The collection features church plate and vestments of various dates, some of which are used in services even today.

Donau-Schifffahrts-Museum (Danube Shipping Museum) (52)

*Marc-Aurel-Ufer
tel. 5 07 58 88, fax 5 07 58 60
www. dsmr.de
Open: daily 10 – 5, from May to Oct.*
This specialist museum is located on two old ships. Firstly, there is the 'Ruthof'/'Ersekcsanád', a steam-powered tug with side paddles. Built in Regensburg in 1922, it houses an interesting exhibition about shipping on the Danube. The second vessel is the 'Freudenau', a motorised tug built further along the Danube in Linz in 1942. The 'Freudenau' is in its original state and is fully functional.

Fürst Thurn und Taxis Schlossmuseum mit Kreuzgang St. Emmeram (Palace Museum and St Emmeram's Cloisters) (53)

Emmeramsplatz 5
tel. 5 04 81 33, fax 5 04 81 40
www.thurnundtaxis.de
Access only during guided tours
Open: April to Oct – tours at 11, 2, 3 and 4 (also at 10 and 1 on Sat, Sun and hols); Nov to March: tours on Sat, Sun and hols at 10, 11, 2 and 3 (10th – 28th of Nov: Mon to Fri at 2.30). Special opening times in the Christmas holidays.

Visitors are shown, firstly, the cloisters of the former Benedictine monastery of St Emmeram, the oldest part of the palace, with its four wings and the two-storey, neo-Gothic Thurn and Taxis family crypt built in 1841 and, secondly, the palace's public and residential apartments, which contain many magnificent 19th-century furnishings as well as some brought from the family's older residences.

Fürst Thurn und Taxis Marstallmuseum (Coach House Museum) (54)

For address see left.
Opening times on enquiry

The building that used to house the stables and an indoor riding-school now contains an exhibition of coaches, sleighs, sedan chairs and ceremonial livery, the private property of the Thurn and Taxis family. The items on show date from the 17th to the 20th centuries.

Fürstliche Schatzkammer (Prince's Treasury) (54)

For address see left.
www.regensburg.de
Open: Mon – Fri 11 – 5 from April to Oct, Sat, Sun, hols 10 – 5. Nov to March only Sat, Sun, hols 10 – 5.

Since 1998 the same building has housed a branch of the Bavarian State Museum displaying precious objects formerly owned by the Thurn and Taxis family. The exhibition includes exquisite specimens of the work of gold-

Elaborately decorated carriages in the Coach House Museum

smiths and silversmiths, porcelain, glassware, furniture and guns and, in addition, a fascinating collection of snuff boxes.

Historisches Museum der Stadt Regensburg (Historical Museum) (55)

Dachauplatz 2 – 4, tel. 5 07 24 48, fax 5 07 44 49; www.regensburg.de Open: Tues – Sun and hols 10 – 4, Thur 10 – 8. Medieval Department: Tue – Fri 12 – 4.
Special tours and group tours arrangement (tel. 5 07 34 42) or museumsfuehrungen@regensburg.de
The former Minorite monastery houses a collection which ranges from prehistoric times to the beginning of the 20th century. What is really exceptional is the fact that virtually all the high-quality exhibits originated in the city or in its immediate surroundings. Many of them are linked with buildings that have been preserved or with well-known local families. Special mention must be made of the Roman and mediaeval sections, but there is also a fine exhibition of paintings of the Danube School (of which Altdorfer was the leading artist) as well as rooms featuring domestic interiors up to the 20th century. A visit cannot fail to be interesting and entertaining.

Mediaeval sculptures and paintings in the Historical Museum

The cloisters at St Emmeram's

Kepler-Gedächtnishaus (Kepler Memorial Museum) (56)

Keplerstraße 5, tel. 5 07 34 42,
fax 5 07 44 49, www.regensburg.de
Open: Sat, Sun and hols from 10.30 –
4. Private tours, dramatised tours
(with actors) by arrangement.
The house where Kepler died
while he was the guest of its
owner contains furniture typical
of wealthy middle-class homes of
the period and also offers a vivid
insight into the work of the
great astronomer through displays of books, instruments and
models.

Kunstforum Ostdeutsche Galerie (Eastern German Art Gallery) (57)

Dr.-Johann-Maier-Straße 5
93049 Regensburg, tel. 29 71 40
fax 2 97 14 33, www.kunstforum.net
Open: Tues – Sun 10 – 5, Thur 10 – 8.
The gallery contains an outstanding collection of paintings, sculpture, graphic art and objets d'art
of the 19th and 20th centuries,
all of which originated in the
eastern parts of Germany or in
Eastern Europe. It includes works
by artists like Lovis Corinth.

Museum St. Ulrich (St Ulrich's Diocesan Museum) (58)

Domplatz 2, tel. 5 16 88,
5 95 32 25 30, fax 5 95 32 25 31
www.bistumsmuseen-regensburg.de
Open: Tue to Sun 10 – 5, from April
to Oct.
The early Gothic church with
its 13th-16th-century wall-pain-
tings contains sacred works of
art dating from the 11th century
to the present-day, all from
churches in Regensburg. The collection includes Altdorfer's
painting of the Virgin Mary.

Naturkundemuseum Ostbayern (Natural History Museum) (59)

Am Prebrunntor 4, tel. 5 07 34 43,
fax 5 07 34 45, www.regensburg.de
Open: Mon 9 – 12; Tues – Fri 9 – 4,
Sun 10 – 5, closed on Sats and hols.
The museum is in an early 19th-
century mansion formerly owned
by the Dukes of Württemberg,
and portrays the development of
life in the eastern Bavarian region from its beginnings. There
is a nature trail with a geological
theme in Herzogspark, the idyllic park right next to the museum.

Reichstagsmuseum (Perpetual Diet Museum) (60)

Old Town Hall, tel. 5 07 34 40
(tourist information office)
www.regensburg.de
Guided tours only. These take place at
the following hours: from April to
Oct: daily every half hour from 9.30
to 12 and from 1.30 to 4; tour in Eng-
lish at 3. Nov 1 – Jan 6 and in Mar:
daily at 10, 11.30, 1.30, 2 (in English),

Entrance of the East German Art Gallery

3 and 3.30. Jan 7 – end of Feb: daily at 10, 11.30, 1.30 and 3. Groups and foreign-language guided tours by prior arrangement (tel. 5 07 34 42). The buildings were used originally as the town hall of Regensburg and occasionally for meetings of the Imperial Diet, from 1663 as the seat of the Perpetual Imperial diet. Today visitors are shown the meeting room of the city council, which later became the prince-electors' meeting room, the ballroom, which later became the Imperial Hall, as well as the places where the princes and the representatives of the Free Imperial Cities met. In two rooms an exhibition of books and prints illustrates the history of the Imperial Diet. The dungeons and inquisition chamber in the cellars are also on show. Not all rooms are always open to the public, since the Old Town Hall is used for weddings, receptions and festive occasions.

Städtische Galerie 'Leerer Beutel' (Municipal Art Gallery at the Leerer Beutel) (61)
Bertoldstraße 9, tel. 5 07 24 40 fax 5 07 44 49, www.regensburg.de Open: Tues – Sun and hols 10 – 4.
Apart from the large exhibition of paintings by 20th-century eastern Bavarian artists which is on constant show in the rooms of the former corn-store, there are varying exhibitions featuring the work of painters from the region, as well as painters from other parts of Germany or the world.

Regensburg's theatre in Bismarckplatz

Art Galleries

Regensburg also offers a large range of privately owned art galleries, often located in rooms featuring mediaeval vaulting, showing a rich variety of art in short-term exhibitions. The current exhibitions are announced in the daily papers and the monthly events brochure published by the city. A small selection of galleries:

Galerie Peter Bäumler (62)
Obere Bachgasse 16, tel. 56 02 63

Galerie Hammer (63)
Untere Bachgasse 6, tel. 56 31 71

Kleine Galerie (64)
Gesandtenstraße 16, tel. 5 13 34

Kunstkabinett (65)
Untere Bachgasse 7, tel. 5 78 56

Kunstkontor Westnerwacht (63)
Weintingergasse 4, tel. 56 07 72

Theatres and Music

Events are announced in the daily newspapers as well as the city's monthly events brochure. Tourist Information in the Old Town Hall can also give details.

Theater Regensburg (Regensburg Theatre) (67)

Bismarckplatz 7, tel. 5 07 44 22
fax 5 07 44 29 (box-office)
www.theaterregensburg.de
season from Sep to mid-July.
Productions include operas, operettas, drama, musicals and ballet, which are performed at the main house in Bismarckplatz, or at the Theater am Haidplatz (a studio theatre) or the open air theatre, both situated in Thon-Dittmer-Palais (p. 53), as well as in the Velodrom (p. 55).

STATT-Theater (68)

Winklergasse 16
tel. 5 33 02, www.statt-theater.de
season from Aug to the end of June.
A smaller, privately run, theatre, specialising in cabaret and similar art forms.

Figurentheater im Stadtpark (Puppet Theatre in the Stadtpark) (69)

Dr.-Johann-Maier-Straße 3
93049 Regensburg, tel. 2 83 28
season from Oct to the end of June.
Productions are enjoyed greatly by audiences of all age groups.

A hotel-room in the Bischhofshof

Performances take place at weekends, special performances by arrangement.

Coccodrillo Theater (70)

Bruderwöhrdstraße 12, tel. 4 61 13 34
www.coccodrillo-theater.de
The theatre that provides a suitable programme for everybody who is young or young at heart!

Leerer Beutel (61)

Bertoldstraße 9
tel. 56 33 75, fax 5 99 97 15
www.jazzclub-regensburg.de
Jazz, live jazz concerts, jazzclub sessions.

Places to Stay

A selection of central hotels with a difference, in various price ranges:

Parkhotel Maximilian (71)

Maximilianstraße 28, tel. 5 68 50
fax 5 29 42, www.maximilian-hotel.de
double rooms from € 129
Situated at the edge of the old city centre overlooking the green ring of avenues which surrounds the centre.

Sorat Insel-Hotel (72)

Müllerstraße 7
tel. 8 10 40, fax 8 10 44 44
www.SORAT-Hotels.com
double rooms from € 135
The rooms on the Danube side of the hotel have beautiful views of the ancient city.

Bischofshof (73)

Krauterermarkt 3, tel. 5 84 60
fax 5 84 61 46, www.hotel-bischofshof.de
double rooms from € 125
Situated in the rooms of the former bishop's palace, this hotel

The Parkhotel Maximilian

has a special wedding suite in the tower of the Roman Porta Praetoria.

Goliath Hotel (74)
Goliathstraße 10
tel. 2 00 09 00, fax. 20 00 90 99
www.hotel-goliath.de
double rooms from € 140
Bed and breakfast hotel with individually designed rooms, roof terrace and spa facilities.

Hotel Karmeliten (75)
Dachauplatz 1
tel. 6 98 49 10, fax. 6 98 49 11 00
www.karmeliten-hotel.de
double rooms from € 74
Re-opened in the former Carmelite monastery in 2007. Rooms from economy to de luxe.

Altstadthotel Arch (76)
Haidplatz 4
tel. 5 86 60, fax 5 86 61 68

www.regensburg-ringhotels.de
double rooms from € 102
One of the old patrician mansions in the city's main square has been turned into a charming hotel.

Münchner Hof (77)
Tändlergasse 9
tel. 5 84 40, fax 56 17 09
www.muenchner-hof.de
double rooms from € 90
In one of the narrow, picturesque alleys in the ancient city.

Hotel d'Orphée (78 and 93)
Wahlenstraße 1 and Untere Bachgasse 8
tel. 59 60 20, fax 59 60 22 22,
www.hotel-orphée.de
double rooms from € 77 to € 115

Budget accommodation
Hotel am Peterstor (79)
Fröhliche-Türken-Straße 12
tel. 5 45 45, fax 5 45 42
double rooms € 58

Spitalgarten (80)
St.-Katharinen-Platz 1, tel. 8 47 74
fax 8 90 31 68, www.spitalgarten.de
double rooms € 54

Jugendherberge (Youth Hostel) (81)
Wöhrdstraße 60
tel. 5 74 02, fax 5 24 11,
www.regensburg.jugendherberge.de
b&b from € 19,40; a YHA member-
ship card is required.

**The Kneitinger brewery's original
pub in Arnulfsplatz**

Food and Drink –
A Feast not only for the Eyes
A selection of restaurants and
pubs in the town centre, which
have typical regional dishes
among their specialities:

For Special Occasions
Rosenpalais (82)
Minoritenweg 20
tel. 5 99 75 79, www.rosenpalais.de
This gourmet restaurant, whose
chefs have won stars for their
cooking, is located on the first
floor of the former summer residence of the Löschenkohl family
(p. 62). The bistro on the ground
floor offers reasonably priced
lunches.

David (83)
Watmarkt 5, tel. 56 18 58
www.hotel-bischofshof.de
Open: daily except for Sun and Mon
from 6 p.m. to midnight.
One of Regensburg's top restaurants: situated on the highest
floor of the Goliathhaus; guests
can enjoy the beautiful view of
the cathedral spires from the
roof terrace.

Bischofshof-Gaststätten
am Dom (73)
Krautermarkt 3, tel. 5 94 10 10
www.bischofshof-am-dom.de
Open: daily from 9 a.m. to midnight.
In the surroundings of the
former bishop's palace, guests
are offered a selection of dishes,
from traditional Bavarian favour-
ites to gourmet cuisine. There is
a lovely beer garden in the courtyard.

Alte Münz (84)
Fischmarkt 7, tel. 5 48 86
www.alte-muenz.de
Open: Mon to Wed from 4 to mid-
night, Thur to Sun from 11 to mid-
night.
Quaint pub, specialising in the
traditional food of the Upper Palatinate.

Good Solid Food – and More
As in the rest of Bavaria, it is the
custom in most of the following
Regensburg pubs to take a seat at
tables where other guests are already sitting and possibly to start
a conversation with them. A

'Stammtisch', a specially designated table for the regulars, is an exception: here an express invitation is necessary before you take a seat.

Kneitinger (85)
Arnulfsplatz 3, tel. 5 24 55
Open: daily from 9.30 a.m. to 1 a.m.
This is the original pub of the Kneitinger brewery (est. 1530), with a time-honoured tradition. Many regulars come here not only for the strong dark beer (Bockbier) but also for the very reasonably priced food.

Hofbräuhaus (86)
Rathausplatz, tel. 5 12 80
Open: daily from 9 a.m. to 1 a.m., closed on Sun between mid May and the end of Sep.
An old Regensburg institution. Guests of all ages, including politicians from the nearby town hall come here for the pub's good food and beer. Don't worry if it seems full, Herr Schafbauer, the publican, will always find you a seat.

Gravenreuther (87)
Hinter der Grieb 10, tel. 5 50 50
www-gravenreuther.de
Open: daily from 10a.m. to midnight.
A typical Bavarian pub with a charming garden.

Dampfnudel-Uli (88)
Watmarkt 4, tel. 5 32 97
Open: Tue to Fri from 10 – 6, Sat 10 – 3.
Here, the speciality is 'Dampfnudeln', large soft yeast dumplings in vanilla sauce (there are half portions for novices!), but Uli Deutzer, the owner, also has

'Dampfnudel-Uli's' speciality

a whole range of other traditional dishes of the region on offer in his pub in the former chapel in the Baumburger Turm, a patrician mansion.

Historische Wurstküche (89)
Beside the Steinerne Brücke (Stone Bridge)
tel. 46 62 10, www.wurstkuchl.de
Open: daily from 8 a.m. to 7 p.m.
The ancient sausage kitchen traditionally serves potato soup, small, spicy Regensburg sausages grilled over a charcoal fire, sauerkraut and sweetish mustard (all home-made) and Schwarzer Kipferl, bread rolls containing caraway from a local bakery. In winter guests sit inside the tiny pub, in summer at tables outside by the river.
The Salzstadel restaurant next door, part of the same business, offers a larger selection of food.

The Spitalgarten, a beergarden in Stadtamhof

Beergardens
The people of Regensburg love to relax in cool, shady beer gardens under chestnut trees. There are a couple of these beer gardens in the old city centre:

Spitalgarten (80)
St.-Katharinen-Platz 1
tel. 8 47 74, www.spitalgarten.de
Open: daily from 10 a.m. to midnight during the beer-garden season.
Home-brewed beers.

Alte Linde (90)
Müllerstraße 1, tel. 8 80 80
Open: daily from 10 a.m. to midnight during the beergarden season.
Beautiful view of the ancient city centre and the Steinerne Brücke.

There are cafés, pubs, bars...
... all over the old city centre.
The following are just a small selection:

Café Goldenes Kreuz (91)
Haidplatz 7, tel. 5 72 32
Open: Mon to Fri from 7 a.m. to 7 p.m. Sat, Sun and hols from 9 a.m. to 7 p.m.
Nicknamed 'Café Important' because people come here to see and be seen.

Konditorei-Café Prock (92)
Kohlenmarkt, tel. 5 44 90

Open: Mon – Sat from 8.30 a.m. – 6.30 p.m. and Sun from 12.30 – 6 p.m.
Famous for its cheesecakes. Lovely courtyard.

Parkcafé Maximilian (71)
Maximilianstraße 28, tel. 5 68 50
Open: daily from 6.30 a.m. to 6 p.m.
Part of the Hotel Maximilian. There is a very pleasant terrace for summer use.

Café-Restaurant Orphée (93)
Untere Bachgasse 8, tel. 5 29 77
Open: daily from 8 a.m. to 1 a.m.
www.hotel-orphee.de
In 1897, a gypsy baron, Alois Finkelsteyn Kornthour, having just fled from Hungary, established a 'Coffee-house and French-style wine-bar' here, and since then the decor has hardly changed. The café sees itself as a home for the arts, a meeting place for free spirits, for different and colourful people; it is popular with Regensburgers of all age groups.

Moccabar (94)
Brückstraße 5, tel. 5 86 55 27
Open: Mon – Sat 8 a.m. – 1 a.m.; Sun 9 a.m. – 1 a.m.
Tables outside in summer with a view of the Stone Bridge

Haus Heuport (95)
Domplatz 7
tel. 5 99 92 97, www.heuport.de
Open: daily from 9 a.m. to 1 a.m.
Café, bar and restaurant in rooms that include the house's Gothic hall. Delightful outdoor seating in the summer with views of the Cathedral or in the sheltered courtyard.

Orphée Café and Restaurant

Galerie (96)
Kohlenmarkt 6
tel. 56 14 08
www.cafe-galerie.de
Open: Mon – Sat 7 a.m – 1 a.m.,
Sun 9 a.m. – 1 a.m.
In summer it also has tables out
in Kohlenmarkt as well as on the
large balcony on the second floor.

Palletti (97)
Pustet-Passage, Gesandtenstraße 6
tel. 5 15 93
Open: Mon to Sat from 8 a.m. to
1 a.m., Sun from 4 p.m. to midnight.
A meeting place for those with
lots of time to spare; mainly
standing-room, except in summer, when there are seats outside.

Tables outside the 'Galerie' in Kohlenmarkt

Clubs

Suite 15 (98)
St. Petersweg 15, tel. 5 04 12 07
Open: Thur 11 p.m. – 3 a.m., Fri – Sat
till 4 a.m.
Thursday: Rock/Indie; Fri: Elek-
tro; Sat: Black/Hiphop/Soul; before every public holiday: disco
music from the 1970s and 1980s.

Scala (99)
Pustet-Passage, Gesandtenstraße 6
tel. 5 22 93
Open: Wed, Thur and Sun from 11 p.m.
to 3 a.m., Sat from 11 p.m. to 4 a.m.
One of the longest existing clubs
in Regensburg; varying styles of
music.

Karma Lounge (100)
Obermünsterstraße 14
Open: Wed from midnight to 3 a.m.,
Fri from 10.30 p.m. to 4 a.m., sat
from midnight to 4 a.m.
Popular disco with varying mu-
sic programme.

**The City Centre Shopping
Experience**
There are shops of all sorts and
sizes in the ancient city centre;
those listed below have unusual
wares on offer, some of them typical of the city or its region.

Handprinted Textiles (101)
Katharieder Bauerndrucke
Kramgasse 6
Linen textiles with typical peas-
ant prints, sold either by the me-
ter or ready worked into table-
mats, cloths, napkins, etc.

Handicrafts (102)
Weichmann, Gesandtenstraße 11
Wide-ranging assortment, mainly
from the firm's own workshops.
An unusual souvenir is a brass
miniature of the 'Bruckmandl'
(p. 36).

Golfing Antiques (103)
Antikhaus Insam
Corner Tändlergasse/Kramgasse
A large selection of prints, en-
gravings etc., on the theme of
golfing, as well as antique golf-
clubs, balls and other objects.

Händlmaier's Mustard

The slightly sweetish mustard has been produced by Händlmaier in Regensburg since about 1920. The jars with their typical red lids are sold by most butchers and grocers in Regensburg but also at outlets worldwide.

Hats (104)

Hutkönig, Krauterermarkt 1
A large selection of hats, including Bavarian-style ones, are offered here. 80% of the felt hats are made in the firm's own workshops.

Chocolates (105)

Prinzess Konditorei, Rathausplatz 2
The Prinzess Confiserie were purveyors of fine chocolates to the Imperial Diet, where the City of Regensburg always provided a small table with sweets. They were so popular that the city soon found this very expensive. All the chocolates today have im-

... seductively sweet

aginative names such as Barbara-Küsse ('Barbara's Kisses'), Don Juan-Kanonenkugeln ('Don Juan's Cannonballs') or Kesse Gloria ('Saucy Gloria').

Schwarzer Kipferl (106)

*Wiener Backhaus Schwarzer
Obere Bachgasse 7*
The popular Schwarzer Kipferl, bread rolls made with rye and caraway, have been baked here according to a traditional recipe for nearly 100 years.

Fashion in the traditional Bavarian style (107)

Pöllinger, Krauterermarkt 4
Leather and Bavarian countrystyle fashion for him, for her and for it.

This and that (108)

*Das Kaufhäuschen
Fröhliche-Türken-Straße 5*
A motley selection of goods from six different suppliers (partly self-made designs) is offered here in confined space.

Pewter and Glass (109)

Wiedamann, Brückstraße 4
A traditional Regensburg business, originally with its own pewter-casting workshop.

Useful information

Information
Tourist Information
*Altes Rathaus (Old Town Hall)
tel. 5 07 44 10, fax 5 07 44 19
www.regensburg.de
Open: Mon to Fri from 9 to 6, Sat
from 9 to 4, Sun and hols 9.30 – 4,
from Nov to Mar 9.30 – 2.30*
For all information on Regens-

burg, brochures, guided tours, the Imperial Diet Museum, accommodation, tickets for events, bus tickets, postcards and stamps.

Tourismusverband Ostbayern (East Bavarian Tourist Board)
Luitpoldstraße 20
tel. 58 53 90, fax 5 85 39 39
www.ostbayern-tourismus.de
For all information on East Bavaria with the exception of information on Regensburg.

Bicycles
Cycling is very popular in Regensburg, which has one of Germany's largest cycling clubs, the Veloclub Ratisbona, which also organises the internationally famous Arber Cycle Marathon each year. The Danube Cycle Path, which is clearly signposted from the source of the Danube as far as Vienna, passes through Regensburg. The Regen Valley Cycle Path and the Naab Valley Cycle Path also intersect here; one can also start out on the Tour de Baroque from here.

Rent a bike/Fahrradverleih/Bike-haus (110)
Bahnhofstraße 17
tel. 5 99 81 94, fax. 56 71 20 91
www.fahrradverleih-regensburg.de
Sales, hire, accessories, repairs.

Guided Tours
Cathedral Tours
Daily at 2 all year round; from May – Sept, also at 10.30 from Mon – Sat. Special tours by arrangement.
tel. 2 98 62 78; fax 2 98 62 80
www.domplatz-5.de
Meeting point and ticket sales Informationszentrum DOMPLATZ 5.

Palace of the Princes of Thurn and Taxis and Coach House Museum
see p. 80

Museums
Special guided tours of the museums are announced in the daily press or the city's monthly events brochure. For groups, such tours in the municipal museums (Historisches Museum, Leerer Beutel, Kepler-Gedächtnismuseum, document Neupfarrplatz and Schnupftabakfabrik) can be arranged on tel. 5 07 34 42 or by email: museumsführungen@regensburg.de

Kepler Memorial Museum
see p. 82

Perpetual Diet Museum
see p. 82

Guided tours of the city
Participants are shown the ancient city centre with its patrician mansions, the refurbished areas, the exterior of the cathedral, the Alte Kapelle, Steinerne Brücke and Porta Praetoria. (Starting point by the Altes Rathaus, duration about 1 1/2 hrs, tickets from the tourist information office, see p. 90*). From Apr to Oct: Mon to Sat at 10.15 and 2.45; from Nov to Mar: Mon to Fri at 2.45 only, Sat at 10.15 and 14.15, Suns and hols all year round at 10.45 and 2.*

Special guided tours and tours in foreign languages
Reservations in writing fax 5 07 44 19 email: tourismus@regensburg.de English-language guided tours from May to Sep at 1.30 on Wed and Sat. From May to Sept: tours on varying

topics at 7 on Tue and Thur; UNESCO
World Heritage Regensburg at 5 on
Fri; tours for children at 10.30 on
Sun; 'Rendez-vous with Europe' at 4
on 1st and 3rd Suns each month;
tour for families 'Veni, vidi, vici' at 6
on 1st Fri each month (starting-place
for this tour is the corner of Ernst-
Reuter-Platz and Maximilianstraße).
Details of other special tours availa-
ble under www.regensburg.de

Dramatised tours
are also offered by 'Stadtmaus'
Bookings: 2 30 36 00, fax 23 03 60 15
www.stadtmaus.de

Tours with 'City Tour'
tel. 6 30 88 13, fax 6 30 88 14
www.city-tour.info
A guided tour in a mini-train is
also available for those unable to
explore the city on foot. (approx.
45 mins).

Events
Annual or biennial events
(further information under
www.regensburg.de):

Easter Week: Bach in the Easter
Week
March: Danube Exhibition (Dult-
platz)
May: Maidult (spring fair / Dult-
platz), Regensburg-Marathon,
Tage Alter Musik (early music fes-
tival)
May-Oct: organ concerts in Mi-
noritenkirche
Mid May – June: schools' theatre
festival in Thon-Dittmer-Hof
June/July: Mediaeval 'Spectaculum'
(Jahninsel), Children's Festival
(Stadtpark)
June – Aug: cathedral organ con-
certs

Mid June: Old Town Festival (every
second year)
Mid July: Jazz Festival (Old Town
squares and courtyards)
July: Thurn and Taxis Palace Festi-
val
September: Herbstdult (autumn
fair / Dultplatz)
November: festival of short films
(Leerer Beutel)
December: Christmas markets in
Neupfarrplatz and Haidplatz
('Lukrezia' Craft Market) (until
Xmas) and Christmas market in
Thurn und Taxis Palace

Out and About with Children
Apart from the special tours for
children that are offered in the
city (p. 92 top), the museums also arrange all kinds of activities
for children at irregular intervals, above all in the school holidays. Particularly recommended
is the Roman Section in the Historical Museum, which gives a
lot of information about the life
of Roman legionaries. Audio
guides (also available in English,
Italian and Czech) make it easy
to explore the displays, also individually. A boat trip on the Danube (p. 93), a picnic on the island
in the Danube beside the Stone
Bridge, a visit to one of Regensburg's swimming-pools or an ice
from one of the ice-cream par-
lours that have existed in Regensburg for almost 100 years – all
these can help to make a visit to
Regensburg memorable. The out-
ings to the Walhalla and to
Weltenburg which are described
above are both suitable for children, too. In the case of the Walhalla trip, a picnic on the grass
beside the Walhalla is to be rec-

ommended in good weather, also
because of the splendid view;
as regards Weltenburg, the suggested round trip from Kelheim
(i.e., on foot via the Hall of Liberation and the archaeological
trail to the Danube, by small
boat across to Weltenburg, and
then back to Kelheim by ship) is
excellent – provided a 5 km walk
is no problem!

Lost Property Office **(111)**
Fundamt, D.-Martin-Luther-Straße 1
tel. 5 07 21 05
Open: Mon to Fri from 8 to 12, Thur
till 1; Mon to Wed 12.30 – 4, Thur
13.30 – 5.30.

Emergency Services
Police
tel. 110

Fire brigade
tel. 112

Ambulance
tel. 1 92 22

Emergency medical service
tel. 1 92 22

ADAC breakdown service
tel. 1802 22 22 22

Car Parking Facilities
Regensburg has a system of elec-
tronic signposts to guide visitors
to free parking lots in one of the
multi-storey carparks or at Donaumarkt. Parking spaces in the
city centre are rare and usually
reserved for residents with special permits.

Assistance for the disabled
A special map of the city centre
with useful information for
those in wheelchairs is available
at the tourist information office.

Pleasure Cruises
Schifffahrtsunternehmen
Klinger GmbH,
Telefon 5 53 59, Fax 56 56 58
Cruises on the Strudel, the stretch of
river adjacent to the town centre, set
out from the Steinerne Brücke, from
Mar to Oct daily from 10 to 4 on the
hour (minimum of 10 participants).
Cruises to the Walhalla leave from the
Steinerne Brücke from Mar to Oct dai-
ly at 10.30 and 2 (minimum of 10
participants). Special cruises by ar-
rangement.

Taxis
There are several taxi ranks in
the city centre, and empty taxis
can also be flagged down.
To call a taxi ring 1 94 10, 5 70 00 or
5 20 52.

Information on events
Events will be announced in the
city's monthly events brochure,
which is available at the tourist
information office (p. 90), or in
the daily papers and in the internet.

Index

Photographic Sources

(the figures refer to page numbers)

altro – die fotoagentur, Regensburg:
2/3, 6, 7, 11, 13, 31, 32 bottom, 33, 37,
39, 48, 49, 55, 61, 62, 64, 73 top,
79 top, 83, 87 top and bottom, 88, 90
and cover pictures

Brandl, Anton J., München: 24 top, 38,
41, 46, 47, 56, 67, 73 bottom, 74

Donau-Schifffahrts-Museum, Regensburg: 79 bottom (Foto: Johann Hei-
duk)

Ferber, Thomas, Regensburg: 15, 24
bottom, 45, 51, 58, 70, 75, 77, 85

Hubel, Achim, Bamberg: 66

Meier, Hanno, Regensburg: 19, 23, 29,
30, 32 top, 42, 43 top and bottom, 52,
53, 57 top and bottom, 81 top, 82

Museen der Stadt Regensburg –
Historisches Museum: 10, 16 bottom,
17, 72, 81 bottom

Presse- und Informationsstelle der
Stadt Regensburg –
Bilddokumentation: 18 (Foto: Peter
Ferstl), 89 (Foto: Horst Hanske)

Stiftung Kneitinger, Regensburg: 86
(Foto: Wolfram Schmidt)

Tourismusverband Ostbayern, Regensburg: 21, 27 (Fotos: Klemens Unger)

Werbeagentur Die Lobby, Regensburg: 84

Widmann, Thomas Peter, Regensburg: 71

Zink, Josef, Regensburg: 16 top, 28,
59, 60, 65, 68

*The author and the publisher are grateful
for permission to publish photographs, etc.
The pictures of the Dominican Church, St
Ulrich's Church and the Cathedral were
kindly furnished by the State Building office. The City Museums have kindly given
permission for the publication of other il-
lustrations.*

Museums

- (48) Brückturmmuseum
- (49) document Neupfarrplatz
- (50) document Schnupftabakfabrik
- (51) Domschatzmuseum
- (52) Donau-Schifffahrts-Museum
- (53) Fürst Thurn und Taxis Schlossmuseum mit Kreuzgang St. Emmeram
- (54) Fürst Thurn und Taxis Marstallmuseum and Fürstliche Schatzkammer
- (55) Historisches Museum der Stadt Regensburg
- (56) Kepler-Gedächtnishaus
- (57) Kunstforum Ostdeutsche Galerie
- (58) Museum St. Ulrich
- (59) Naturkundemuseum Ostbayern
- (60) Reichstagsmuseum
- (61) Städt. Galerie Leerer Beutel
- (62) Galerie Peter Bäumler
- (63) Galerie Ludwig Hammer
- (64) Kleine Galerie
- (65) Kunstkabinett
- (66) Kunstkontor Westnerwacht

Theatres and Music

- (67) Theater Regensburg
- (68) STATT-Theater
- (69) Figurentheater im Stadtpark
- (70) Coccodrillo Theater

Accomodation, Restaurants

- (71) Parkhotel Maximilian
- (72) Sorat Insel-Hotel
- (73) Bischofshof Hotel, Gaststätten
- (74) Goliath Hotel
- (75) Hotel Karmeliten
- (76) Altstadthotel Arch
- (77) Münchner Hof
- (78) Hotel d'Orphée
- (79) Hotel am Peterstor
- (80) Spitalgarten
- (81) Jugendherberge
- (82) Rosenpalais
- (83) David
- (84) Alte Münz
- (85) Kneitinger
- (86) Hofbräuhaus
- (87) Gravenreuther
- (88) Dampfnudel-Uli
- (89) Historische Wurstküche
- (90) Alte Linde
- (91) Café Goldenes Kreuz
- (92) Konditorei-Café Prock
- (93) Café-Restaurant Orphée
- (94) Moccabar
- (95) Haus Heuport
- (96) Galerie
- (97) Palletti
- (98) Suite 15
- (99) Scala
- (100) Karma Lounge

City Centre Shopping

- (101) Katharieder Bauerndrucke
- (102) Kunsthandwerk Weichmann
- (103) Antikhaus Insam – Golfantiquitäten
- (104) Hutkönig
- (105) Prinzess Konditorei
- (106) Backhaus Schwarzer
- (107) Pöllinger Trachtenmoden
- (108) Das Kaufhäuschen
- (109) Wiedamann Zinn und Glas
- (110) Rent a Bike / Fahrradverleih
- (111) Fundamt, Lost Property